FOREWORD

NAVY AIR COMBAT FIGHTER

US Navy/Liz Goettee

THE HISTORY OF the F/A-18 Hornet strike fighter dates to May 1974. That signified the launch of the Navy Air Combat Fighter programme and the selection of the Northrop YF-17 Cobra, originally developed for the US Air Force Light Weight Fighter programme. The redesign of the Cobra was undertaken in a joint effort between Northrop and its partner, McDonnell Douglas which had the experience of designing and building the carrier-capable F-4 Phantom.

McDonnell Douglas' Model 267 was a heavily modified YF-17, later designated the F-18A and named the Hornet. The first pre-production F-18A prototype made the type's maiden flight from St Louis-Lambert Field, Missouri on November 18, 1978.

As a major design series aircraft, the F-18 was manufactured in single-seat and two-seat configurations, originally dubbed the F-18A and TF-18 respectively. Designations were changed to F/A-18A and F/A-18B to reflect the aircraft's combined fighter and attack capability. The first production single-set F/A-18A made its maiden flight from St Louis-Lambert Field on April 12, 1980.

Much of the developmental flight testing was undertaken by Naval Air System Command's Air Test and Evaluation Squadron 23 (VX-23) at Patuxent River, Maryland. Operational flight testing started in 1981, conducted by the then VX-4 based at Point Mugu, and VX-5 based at China Lake, both in southern California. In April 1981, the first operational Hornets were assigned to Strike Fighter Squadron 125 (VFA-125) 'Rough Raiders' based at Lemoore, California.

Much has happened to the F/A-18 Hornet since the early days: development of the F/A-18C and F/A-18D Hornets, followed by the E- and F-model Super Hornets, and ultimately the EA-18G Growler designed and built specifically for the electronic attack mission. Australia, Canada, Finland, Kuwait, Malaysia, Spain, and Switzerland all procured versions of the F/A-18, while Australia and Kuwait subsequently procured Super Hornets.

Whatever your interest in aviation, F/A-18 Hornet - America's Multirole Naval Jet, is packed full of features about Classic Hornet, Super Hornet and Growler aircraft operated by the US Navy and the US Marine Corps.

Mark Ayton
Mark Ayton
Editor

WWW.KEY.AERO 3

CONTENTS

06 INTRODUCTION
Mark Ayton details the evolution of the McDonnell Douglas F/A-18 Hornet.

08 CLASSIC HORNETS
We provide details of the classic F/A-18 Hornet family using unclassified excerpts from the US Navy F/A-18 Hornet flight manual.

22 HORNET: PREPARING FOR RETIREMENT
Lon Nordeen and Mark Ayton provide an overview of the problems faced by the US Marine Corps to sustain its F/A-18 Hornet fleet through to final retirement in FY2030.

30 SUPER HORNET
We chart the development of the F/A-18 Super Hornet series of strike fighters.

50 MISSILES AND MUNITIONS
Details of the F/A-18 Super Hornet's missile and munitions arsenal, its operational test programme, the Block II, and the latest test programmes of the Block III variant.

66 SUPER HORNET FLEET AND TRAINING SQUADRONS
Mark Ayton outlines the US Navy's Super Hornet force structure and its training squadrons assigned to the Atlantic and Pacific fleets.

70 SUPER HORNET RENOVATION
Lon Nordeen details Boeing's Service Life Modification Program currently underway to sustain the US Navy's Super Hornet fleet.

78 BEEPS AND SQUEAKS
Mark Ayton charts the development of the EA-18G Growler electronic attack aircraft.

92 TACTICAL JAMMING SYSTEMS
An overview of the EA-18G Growler's ALQ-99 and ALQ-249 tactical jamming systems.

100 VIKINGS: THE GROWLER SCHOOLHOUSE
Mark Ayton details the training mission of Electronic Attack Squadron 129, the schoolhouse and repository of electronic attack in the US Navy.

US Navy

US Navy/Mass Communication Specialist Gretchen Roth

US Navy/Mass Communication Specialist Travis Alston

Editor
Mark Ayton
Senior editor, specials
Roger Mortimer
roger.mortimer@keypublishing.com
Design
Dominique Maynard
Head designer
Steve Donovan
Advertising Sales Manager
Brodie Baxter
brodie.baxter@keypublishing.com
01780 755131
Advertising Production
Rebecca Antoniades
rebecca.antoniades@keypublishing.com

SUBSCRIPTION/MAIL ORDER
Key Publishing Ltd, PO Box 300,
Stamford, Lincs, PE9 1NA
Tel 01780 480404
Fax 01780 757812
Email subs@keypublishing.com
Mail Order
orders@keypublishing.com
www.keypublishing.com/shop

PUBLISHING
Group CEO
Adrian Cox
Publisher
Mark Elliott
Head of Publishing
Finbarr O'Reilly
Chief Publishing Officer
Jonathan Jackson

Key Publishing Ltd, PO Box 100,
Stamford, Lincs, PE9 1XP
01780 755131
www.keypublishing.com

PRINTING
Precision Colour Printing Ltd,
Haldane, Halesfield 1,
Telford, Shropshire. TF7 4QQ

DISTRIBUTION
Seymour Distribution Ltd,
2 Poultry Avenue,
London, EC1A 9PU
Enquiries 02074 294000.

We are unable to guarantee the bonafides of any of our advertisers. Readers are strongly recommended to take their own precautions before parting with any information or item of value, including, but not limited to money, manuscripts, photographs or personal information in response to any advertisements within this publication.

© Key Publishing Ltd 2022
All rights reserved. No part of this magazine may be reproduced or transmitted in any form by any means, electronic or mechanical, including photocopying, recording or by any information storage and retrieval system, without prior permission in writing from the copyright owner. Multiple copying of the contents of the magazine without prior written approval is not permitted.

WWW.KEY.AERO

INTRODUCTION

DECADES OF EVOLUTION

Mark Ayton outlines the evolution of the McDonnell Douglas F/A-18 Hornet from its original incarnation, through the development of the Super Hornet and Growler, to today's advanced versions.

THE MCDONNELL DOUGLAS F/A-18 Hornet is a carrier-capable strike fighter. Since YF-18A Full Scale Development aircraft BuNo 160777 made the type's first arrested landing on the flight deck of the USS *America* (CV 66) in October 1979, F/A-18s have deployed onboard America's fleet of super carriers. Right now, F/A-18 Super Hornet strike fighters are operating from the flight decks of aircraft carriers across the globe. Based on the author's experience, watching a 50,000lb Super Hornet flying at 130kts catch a 1.5in thick cable and arrest on the flight deck within 350ft is a sight to behold.

When the F/A-18 entered service with Marine Fighter Attack Squadron 314 (VMFA-314) 'Black Knights' in January 1983, it did so with a then eye-watering specification: it was the first naval tactical aircraft designed to carry out both air-to-air and air-to-ground missions; the first to have carbon fibre wings and the first to use digital fly-by-wire flight controls. Between February and August 1985, Strike Fighter Squadron 25 (VFA-25) 'Fist of the Fleet' and VFA-113 'Stingers' undertook the US Navy's first F/A-18 carrier deployment on board USS *Constellation* (CV 64) embarked as the new tip of the spear within, the now dis-established, Carrier Air Wing 14.

F/A-18C Hornet Characteristics	
Length	56ft (17.07m)
Height	15ft 4in (4.67m)
Wingspan	40ft 5in (12.32m)
Max take-off weight	51,900lb (23,500kg)
Airspeed	Mach 1.7+
Ceiling	50,000ft plus (15,240m)
Combat range	1,089nm (2,016km)
Propulsion	Two F404-GE-402 enhanced performance turbofan engines each rated at 17,700lb

YF-18A Full Scale Development aircraft BuNo 160775 made the type's maiden flight from St Louis-Lambert Field on November 18, 1978, following its roll-out from the McDonnell Douglas plant on September 13. **McDonnell Douglas**

YF-18A Full Scale Development aircraft BuNo 160775 seen with its landing gears retracted on an early test flight. **Naval Air Systems Command**

F/A-18E and F/A-18F Super Hornet Characteristics

Length	60ft 3in (18.36m)
Height	16ft (4.88m)
Wingspan	44ft 10in (13.66m)
Max take-off weight	66,000lb (29,937kg)
Airspeed	Mach 1.8+
Ceiling	50,000ft plus (15,240m)
Combat range	1,275nm (2,361km)
Propulsion	Two F414-GE-400 turbofan engines each rated at 22,000lb

In early October 1985, USS *Coral Sea* (CV 43) departed Naval Base Norfolk, Virginia with the now dis-established Carrier Air Wing 13. This was a notable deployment involving the oldest aircraft carrier in the US Navy's fleet and the first with a carrier air wing comprising four F/A-18A Hornet-equipped squadrons, two of which were US Marine Corps units. On April 15, 1986, Hornets operating from the USS *Coral Sea* undertook the type's first combat strikes on Libyan air defences in support of Operation Prairie Fire and targets in Benghazi as part of Operation El Dorado Canyon.

The F/A-18's evolution continued with the development and service entry of the F/A-18C and F/A-18D models, followed by the larger and more powerful Super Hornet, the first of which, a single-seat Block I F/A-18E model, made the type's first flight from St Louis-Lambert Field in November 1995.

Service entry with the US Navy followed in 1999 with Strike Fighter Wing Pacific's Strike Fighter Squadron 122 (VFA-122) 'Flying Eagles', the Super Hornet Fleet Replacement Squadron (FRS) based at Naval Air Station Lemoore, California. Initial operational capability was achieved with Lemoore-based VFA-115 'Eagles' in September 2001. While underway in the Persian Gulf, on November 6, 2002, and while assigned to CVW-14 embarked on the USS *Abraham Lincoln* (CVN 72), VFA-115 flew the Super Hornet's first combat mission with strikes against two targets at Al Kut, Iraq in support of Operation Southern Watch.

The first major upgrade to the Super Hornet, dubbed the Block II, featured the Raytheon APG-79 active electronically scanned array (AESA) radar. First delivered in April 2005, the Block II was the world's first fighter to enter frontline service equipped with a tactical multimode AESA radar. Lead unit was F/A-18F-equipped Strike Fighter Squadron 213 (VFA-213) 'Black Lions' based at Naval Air Station Oceana, Virginia. Today, all CVW-assigned Super Hornet squadrons operate Block II jets.

As a major design series aircraft, the F/A-18's evolution continued with the electronic attack variant designated the EA-18G and named the Growler. The first of two-system design and development aircraft, EA-1, made the type's maiden flight from St Louis-Lambert Field on August 15, 2006.

Today, all Electronic Attack Squadrons (VAQs) are based at Naval Air Station Whidbey Island, Washington where the FRS accepted the first fleet aircraft, VAQ-129 on June 3, 2008.

On June 18, 2017, Lieutenant Commander Michael Tremel assigned to Strike Fighter Squadron 87 (VFA-87) 'Golden Warriors' flying an F/A-18E shot down a Syrian Air Force Su-22 fighter-bomber, the first air-to-air kill by a Super Hornet.

Today, Boeing and Naval Air Systems Command are developing the most capable variant of the F/A-18 series to date, the Block III Super Hornet. The variant's maiden flight took place from St Louis-Lambert Field on June 4, 2020, with F/A-18F c/n F287. More recently, Naval Air Systems Command received the first Block III Super Hornet on September 27, 2021. Naval Air Systems Command's Air Test and Evaluation Squadrons 23 (VX-23) 'Salty Dogs' and VX-31 'Dust Devils' are currently flying Block III Super Hornets in the variant's flight test programme which is scheduled to be completed by Q2 FY2024.

YF-18A Full Scale Development aircraft BuNo 160777 a moment before making the type's first arrested landing on the flight deck of the USS *America* (CV 66) in October 1979. **Naval Air Systems Command**

EA-18G Growler Characteristics

Length	60ft 2in (18.34m)
Height	16ft (4.88m)
Wingspan	44ft 10in (13.66m)
Recovery weight	48,000lb (21,772kg)
Ceiling	50,000ft (15,240m)
Combat range	850nm (1,574km) plus
Propulsion	Two F414-GE-400 turbofan engines each rated at 22,000lb

F/A-18 HORNET

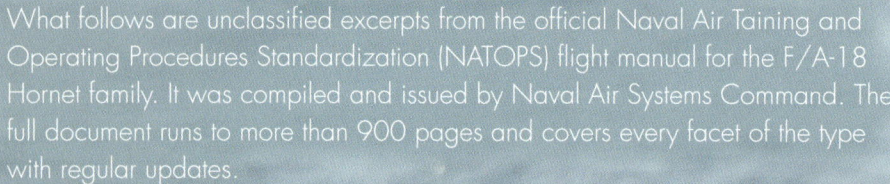

What follows are unclassified excerpts from the official Naval Air Taining and Operating Procedures Standardization (NATOPS) flight manual for the F/A-18 Hornet family. It was compiled and issued by Naval Air Systems Command. The full document runs to more than 900 pages and covers every facet of the type with regular updates.

THE F/A-18A and F/A-18C Hornet are single-seat fighter/attack aircraft built by McDonnell Douglas Aerospace. They are powered by two General Electric F404-GE-400 or F404-GE-402 (enhanced performance) turbofan engines with afterburner. The aircraft features a variable camber mid-wing with leading edge extensions (LEX) mounted on each side of the fuselage from the wing roots to just forward of the windshield. The twin vertical stabilisers are angled outboard 20° from the vertical. The wings have hydraulically actuated leading edge and trailing edge flaps and ailerons. The twin rudders and differential stabilators are also hydraulically actuated. The speed brake is mounted on the top side of the aft fuselage between the vertical stabilisers. The pressurized cockpit is enclosed by an electrically operated clam shell canopy. An aircraft mounted auxiliary power unit (APU) is used to start the engines. On the ground, the APU may be used to supply air conditioning or electrical and hydraulic power to the aircraft systems.

Mission
The aircraft has an all-weather intercept, identify, destroy, and ground attack capability. Air-to-air armament normally comprises AIM-7, AIM-9, and AIM-120 missiles and a 20mm gun. Various air-to-ground stores can be carried. Mission range can be extended with the addition of up to three external fuel tanks.

Engines
The aircraft is powered by two General Electric engines: F404-GE-400 in Lot 13 and below and either F404-GE-400 or F404-GE-402 in Lot 14 and above. The military thrust of each F404-GE-400 engine is approximately 10,700lb with maximum afterburner thrust in the 16,000lb-class. The military thrust of each F404-GE-402 engine is approximately 10,900lb with maximum afterburner thrust in the 18,000lb-class. The aircraft thrust-to-weight ratio is in the 1 to 1 class.

The engine is a low bypass axial-flow turbofan with afterburner. The three-stage fan (low pressure compressor) is driven by a single stage turbine. Approximately one-third of the fan discharge air is bypassed to the afterburner for combustion and cooling. The seven-stage high pressure compressor is also driven by a single stage turbine. The first and second stage compressor stators are variable. Fourth stage compressor air is used by the engine anti-ice system. A set of variable inlet guide vanes are mounted in front of both the fan and compressor to direct the inlet air at the best angle for the existing engine operation. Atomized fuel and compressor discharge air is mixed and ignited in the combustion chamber. These ignited gases then pass through the compressor and fan turbines and out the engine exhaust. Afterburner operation uses added atomized fuel mixed with the combustion discharge gases and the bypass fan discharge air to produce additional thrust. The electrical control assembly, variable exhaust nozzles, main fuel control, and afterburner fuel control provide coordinated operation of the engine through every part of its envelope. The engine accessory gearbox, driven by the compressor rotor, powers the lubrication and scavenge oil pumps, variable exhaust nozzle power unit, alternator, main fuel pump and control, and afterburner fuel pump and control. An aircraft-mounted auxiliary power unit is used to start the engines.

Air Induction System
The air induction system is designed to provide compatible air to the engine. The system uses a fixed geometry compression ramp, a fuselage boundary layer diverter system and a ramp boundary layer bleed system. The compressor ramp provides the correct oblique shock wave for inlet air at most Mach numbers.

The fuselage boundary layer diverter system prevents low energy air from entering the inlets. This low energy air is diverted below the fuselage. The rear part of the compression ramp is porous to prevent this boundary layer air from entering the inlet. Part of the boundary layer air is bled through a fixed area outlet into the fuselage boundary layer diverter channel. The other part exits on top of the wing through inlet duct doors, when open.

Electrically operated inlet duct doors (one for each inlet) automatically open at Mach 1.33 (accelerating) and close at Mach 1.23 (decelerating). The doors are controlled by the flight control computer.

Engine Control System
The engine control system consists of the throttle, main fuel control, electrical control assembly (ECA) and afterburner fuel control. Throttle movement is mechanically transmitted to a power lever control which acts as a power booster and positions the main fuel control. If the automatic throttle control is engaged, it schedules the power lever control for existing engine power requirements and the throttle follows this movement. Below MIL power, throttle movement and compressor inlet temperature (through the main fuel control) control the compressor speed (rpm). At MIL and above, fan speed is controlled by the ECA as a function of inlet temperature. At and above MIL power, the ECA senses engine and aircraft parameters, computes engine schedules and maintains engine limits.

Afterburner Fuel Control
The afterburner fuel control schedules fuel flow to the pilot spraybar and main spraybars. When the throttle is advanced to afterburner,

An F/A-18C Hornet assigned to Strike Fighter Squadron 131 (VFA-131) 'Wildcats' launches off the flight deck of the aircraft carrier USS Dwight Eisenhower (CVN 69). **US Navy/Mass Communication Specialist Andrew Schneider**

We provide details of the classic F/A-18 Hornet family using unclassified excerpts from the official US Navy flight manual.

CLASSIC HORNETS

F/A-18 HORNET

An F/A-18C Hornet assigned to Marine Fighter Attack Squadron 323 (VMFA-323) 'Death Rattlers' over the ramp, the start of the flight deck, at the stern of the ship, in this case USS Nimitz (CVN 68). **US Navy/Mass Communication Specialist Siobhana McEwen**

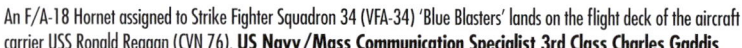

An F/A-18 Hornet assigned to Strike Fighter Squadron 34 (VFA-34) 'Blue Blasters' lands on the flight deck of the aircraft carrier USS Ronald Reagan (CVN 76). **US Navy/Mass Communication Specialist 3rd Class Charles Gaddis**

ignition is turned on, the exhaust nozzle opens slightly above the MIL position, the low-pressure turbine discharge temperature schedule is temporarily reset to a lower value, and afterburner pilot spraybar fuel flow and minimum afterburner main fuel flow begins. When afterburner light-off is detected, ignition is turned off and afterburner main fuel flow increases to the level selected by the throttle position. Since main fuel flow is withheld until a positive light-off is attained, a hard light should not occur.

A successful afterburner light-off is indicated by the exhaust nozzle opening to a position greater than MIL (scheduled as a function of power lever angle or PLA). Nozzle position at MAX power is approximately 50% greater than MIL.

Automatic Throttle Control

The automatic throttle control (ATC) is a two-mode system that automatically maintains angle of attack (approach mode) or airspeed (cruise mode) by modulating engine thrust in the range of flight idle through military. Automatic transition between the two modes or single-engine engagement is not possible. When either mode is engaged, the ECS air to the torque boosters is shut off, the throttles are initially back driven, a stop is extended in the power lever control (PLC) to limit throttle travel from flight idle to MIL, and an ATC advisory is displayed on the head-up display (HUD).

Fuel System

Fuel is carried internally in four interconnected fuselage tanks and two internal wing (wet) tanks. External fuel is carried in 315 or 330-gallon tanks which may be mounted on the centreline and/or inboard wing station pylons. A fuel quantity indicating system provides fuel quantity indications in pounds. All tanks may be refuelled on the ground through a single pressure refuelling point. Airborne, they can be refuelled through the aerial refuelling probe. The internal wing tanks 1 and 4 are transfer tanks. Tanks 2 and 3 are engine feed tanks. The tanks are arranged so internal fuel gravity transfers (at a reduced rate) even if the transfer pumps fail. Regulated engine bleed air pressure transfers fuel from the external tanks and also provides a positive pressure on all internal fuel tanks. Float type fuel level control valves control refuelling of all tanks. These same valves are used to control transfer from the internal wing tanks to tanks 1 and 4 in F/A-18A and F/A-18B variants, and to tank 2 from the left-wing tank and to tank 3 from the right-wing tank in F/A-18C and F/A-18D variants. Jet level sensors are used to control transfer from tanks 1 and 4 to tanks 2 and 3. All internal and external tanks except tanks 2 and 3 (and internal wing tanks in F/A-18C and F/A-18D variants) may be dumped overboard from an outlet in each vertical fin. All internal fuel tanks are vented through the vent outlet in each vertical fin. The external tanks are vented through the vent outlets in their individual tanks.

The internal wing tanks contain foam for fire/explosion protection. The lower section of the feed tanks is self-sealing for 'get home' protection. Fuel lines are routed inside the tanks where possible. Fuel feed lines in the main landing gear wells are wrapped with a self-sealing protective shell.

Fuel Tank Pressurization and Vent

The pressurization and vent system provides regulated engine bleed air pressure to all internal tanks to prevent fuel boil-off at altitude and to the external tanks for fuel transfer. The system also provides pressure relief of the fuel tanks during climbs and vacuum relief of the fuel tanks during descent if the pressurization system fails. All tanks are pressurized any time engine bleed air is available, electrical power is on, weight is off the main gear, the air refuelling probe is retracted.

The internal tanks vent into the fuselage vent tank which in turn is vented through the vertical fin vent tanks to an outlet in each vertical fin. Any fuel in the vertical fin vent tank returns to the vent tank by gravity flow. Any fuel that accumulates in the vent tank is returned to tanks 2 and 3 by scavenge pumps.

Internal Fuel Transfer: F/A-18A and F/A-18B

Normal fuel transfer is accomplished by ejector pumps powered by motive flow. Motive flow pressure is produced by two motive flow/boost pumps, each driven by an airframe mounted accessory drive (AMAD). If an AMAD or pump failure occurs, the other pump produces sufficient motive flow pressure to power all the ejector pumps. The ejector pumps in the internal wing tanks automatically transfer fuel to tanks 1 and 4 when the fuel level control valves in these two tanks open. The ejector pumps in tanks 1 and 4 transfer fuel to tanks 2 and 3 when the jet level sensors in the feed tanks are uncovered, allowing their transfer control valves to open.

After tank 1, tank 4 or a wing tank empties, fuel low level floats shut off motive flow to the ejector pump in that tank.

Internal Fuel Transfer: F/A-18C and F/A-18D

Normal fuel transfer is accomplished by motive flow powered ejector pumps in the internal wing tanks and turbine-driven pumps in tanks 1 and 4. Motive flow pressure is produced by two motive flow/boost pumps, each driven by an airframe mounted accessory drive (AMAD). Two separate motive flow systems exist, with the right AMAD pump powering the transfer pumps in the right wing and tank 4 and the left AMAD pump powering the transfer pumps in the left wing and tank 1. If an AMAD or motive flow/boost pump failure occurs, a cross-motive valve opens, allowing the good side to power all the transfer pumps. The wings transfer first, and transfer is controlled by the feed tank fuel level control valves. The ejector pumps transfer left-wing fuel to tank 2 and right-wing fuel to tank 3. When tanks 2 and 3 deplete to jet level sensor control range, the turbine-driven pumps in tanks 1 and 4 transfer fuel to tanks 2 and 3 when the sensors are uncovered, allowing the transfer control valves to open. Fuel transfer

A US Marine Corps F/A-18D Hornet receives fuel from a US Air Force KC-10A Extender assigned to the 908th Expeditionary Air Refueling Squadron. **US Air Force/SSgt Daniel Snider**

F/A-18 HORNET

An F/A-18C Hornet assigned to Strike Fighter Squadron 94 (VFA-94) 'Mighty Shrikes' banks away from a US Air Force KC-10A Extender after aerial refuelling. **US Air Force/TSgt Rob Tabor**

from tanks 1 and 4 is shut off during negative g flight. After tank 1 or tank 4 empties, fuel low level floats shut off motive flow to the turbine-driven pump in that tank. The ejector pumps do not shut off when the internal wing tanks are empty.

External Transfer

External fuel is transferred by conditioned engine bleed air pressure. A single regulator supplies pressurization to all installed external tanks when weight is off the wheels, the air refuelling probe is retracted, and in F/A-18A and F/A-18B aircraft, the arrestor hook handle is up or in F/A-18C and F/A-18D aircraft, either the arrestor hook handle or landing gear handle is up. Once the external tanks are pressurized, shut-off valves controlled by the external tank fuel control switches provide selection of fuel transfer from either the external wing tanks only, the external centreline tank only or all three external tanks at the same time. All external tanks can be pressurized any time either external tank fuel control switch is in ORIDE (arresting hook handle must be up in F/A-18A and F/A-18B aircraft). On F/A-18C and F/A-18D aircraft, selecting ORIDE also overrides any signal data computer (SDC) stop transfer command. With the external tanks pressurized, fuel transfers when the fuel low caution is displayed (the air refuelling probe must be retracted in F/A-18C and F/A-18D aircraft), regardless of the position of the external tank fuel control switches.

A hydraulically operated inflight refuelling probe is positioned on the right side of the fuselage forward of the windshield. The probe is extended and retracted by the hydraulic system and controlled by a guarded probe switch on the fuel panel. An emergency extension system uses APU accumulator pressure to extend the probe.

Auxiliary Power Unit

The auxiliary power unit (APU) is a small aircraft mounted gas turbine engine used to generate a source of air to power the air turbine starter(s) or to augment the engine bleed air supply to the ECS. It is situated on the underside of the fuselage between the engines, with both intake and exhaust facing

F/A-18D Hornets assigned to Marine All Weather Fighter Attack Squadron 242 (VMFA(AW)-242) 'Bats' prepare for take-off from Andersen Air Force Base, Guam, during Cope North 2020, an annual US Pacific Air Forces multilateral field training exercise. **US Marine Corps/LCpl Jackson Ricker**

downwards. A hydraulic motor powered by the APU accumulator, normally charged by the hydraulic system designated HYD 2B, is used to start the APU. A hand pump may be used to charge the accumulator. The aircraft battery provides electrical power for the APU ignition and start control circuits. The APU uses aircraft fuel.

Electrical Power Supply Systems

The electrical power supply system consists of two AC generators, two transformer-rectifiers, two batteries with integral battery chargers on aircraft BuNo 161353 through BuNo 161528, or a single battery charger transformer-rectifier unit (TRU) which charges both batteries on aircraft BuNo 161702 and upward, and a power distribution (bus) system. External electrical power can be applied to the bus system on the ground. In the absence of external electrical power, battery power is provided for engine starts, whether using the onboard APU or external air.

Hydraulic Power Supply System

Hydraulic power is supplied by two separate systems, HYD 1 and HYD 2. Each system consists of two hydraulic circuits (circuit A and circuit B). The two hydraulic systems are identical except for the fluid supply line from the hydraulic system 2 reservoir assembly to the APU hydraulic hand pump. System 1 on the left-hand side, provides power to the primary flight control surface actuators exclusively. System 2 on the right-hand side, also provides power to the primary flight control actuators and additionally supplies power to the speed brake and non-flight control actuators.

Redundancy to the flight control actuators is achieved either by simultaneously pressurizing the actuator from both systems or by supplying pressure to the actuator from one system while the other system is in a back-up mode.

Primary Flight Controls

The primary flight controls are the ailerons, twin rudders, differential/collective leading-edge flaps, differential/collective trailing edge flaps and differential/collective stabilators. Stick and rudder feel are provided by spring cartridges. Although there is no aerodynamic feedback to the stick and rudder pedals, the effect is simulated by flight control computer scheduling of control surface deflection versus pilot input as a function of flight conditions. Normally, inputs to the hydraulic actuators are provided by the two flight control computers (FCC A and FCC B) through the full authority control augmentation system (CAS). A direct electrical link (DEL) automatically backs up the CAS. DEL is normally a digital system but has an analogue mode for backup aileron and rudder control. If digital DEL fails, a mechanical link (MECH) automatically provides roll and pitch control through a direct mechanical input from the stick to the stabilator actuators. MECH bypasses both flight control computers and the stabilator actuator servo valves.

Multiple redundant paths ensure that single failures have no effect and multiple failures have minimum effect on control.

Hydraulic Power

Hydraulic power is supplied by HYD 1 and HYD 2 to all primary flight control actuators. Failure of either HYD 1 or HYD 2 does not affect flight control when configured in flaps auto up, however, failure of either hydraulic system when configured flaps half or flaps full may cause an uncommanded yaw and roll transient as the switching valves cycle. The uncommanded yaw and roll may be severe under certain situations such as single engine and high or low speed flight. The uncommanded yaw and roll transient may last three to six seconds.

The system is arranged to minimise the probability of loss of control to any surface or the loss of control of one surface due to catastrophic damage to the lines or actuator powering any other surface.

G Limiter

The g limiter prevents exceeding the aircraft positive g limit under most conditions while permitting full symmetrical and unsymmetrical (rolling) manoeuvring. The reference for symmetrical pilot commands is the aircraft design load (+7.5g at 32,357lb gross weight). Unsymmetrical pilot command limits are dependent on lateral stick position and vary from the symmetrical limit with small lateral stick displacement to 80% of the symmetrical limit with full lateral stick displacement. A g limiter override feature allows an increase in the command limit g for emergency use.

Below 44,000lb gross weight, the positive symmetrical command limit is calculated based on fuel state and stores loading. Above 44,000lb gross weight, the positive symmetrical command limit is fixed at +5.5g. The negative symmetrical command limit is fixed at -3.0g at all gross weights and stores loading. Longitudinal stick displacement required to achieve command limit g varies with airspeed and gross weight. When the command limit g is reached, additional aft stick does not increase g. The positive command limit g is reduced when decelerating through the transonic region. This reduction may be as much as 1.0g providing the available g is not reduced below +5.0g.

Spin Recovery System

The spin recovery system, when engaged, puts the flight controls in a spin recovery mode

Two F/A-18Ds assigned to the then Marine All Weather Fighter Attack Squadron 121 (VMFA(AW)-121) 'Green Knights' at Al Asad Air Base, Iraq, in April 2007. **US Marine Corps/Cpl Sheila Brooks**

(SRM). This mode, unlike CAS, gives the pilot full aileron, rudder and stabilator authority without any control surface interconnects and all rate and acceleration feedbacks are removed. The leading-edge flaps are driven to 33° ±1° down and the trailing edge flaps are driven to 0° ±1°.

Flight Control Computers

Two flight control computers (FCC A and FCC B) provide the computations which determine the flight characteristics. Electrical signals generated by movement of the stick grip and rudder pedals are transmitted to both FCC (each signal on four different channels). The computers use the pilot inputs and inputs from various aircraft and internal sensors to determine proper outputs to the control actuators for desired aircraft response. The multiple channel inputs and outputs are continuously monitored by the FCC for agreement. When there is disagreement, the erroneous signal is discarded or, if this cannot be determined, the control system is automatically switched to a degraded mode which does not use that signal. For survivability, one channel from each computer is routed through the upper part of the aircraft and the other channel is routed through the lower part. The stabilator and trailing edge flap servos receive four channel signals from the FCC. The aileron, rudder, and leading-edge flap servos receive two channel signals. FCC A is powered by the essential 28-volt DC bus. FCC B is powered by the right 28-volt DC bus. Both computers are normally cooled by avionics air, but ram air can be selected for FCC A cooling. The FCCs are provided with separate power inputs which are connected directly to the battery/charger. FCC A is connected to the emergency battery and the FCC B is connected to the utility battery. Should a power interruption occur on the main DC bus, sensors within the flight control computer automatically switch to the backup power source for up to seven seconds. This ensures the flight control computers have uninterrupted power to maintain full flight control electronic system performance during all predictable bus s witching transients.

Speedbrake

The speedbrake is mounted between the vertical stabilisers. It is controlled by a throttle mounted switch using left 28-volt DC bus power. It is powered by the HYD 2A system.

Airborne, when in the auto flaps up mode, the speedbrake automatically retracts above 6.0g or above 28° AOA and, when not in the auto flaps up mode, below 250kts.

Automatic Flight Control System

The automatic flight control system (autopilot) has two basic modes: pilot relief and data link. The pilot relief mode consists of heading hold, heading select, attitude hold, barometric altitude hold, radar altitude hold, control stick steering (CSS) and coupled steering. The data link mode consists of automatic carrier landing (ACL), precision course direction, and vector approach.

Before any mode can be selected bank must be less than or equal to 70°, pitch must be less than or equal to 45°, and the autopilot pushbutton must be pressed.

Landing Gear

The landing system is made up of the landing gear, nosewheel steering, brakes, launch bar, and arresting hook. The landing gear system is electrically controlled and hydraulically operated. The main gear is retracted aft into the fuselage and the nose gear is retracted forward. When the gear is extended, all gear doors remain open.

Nosewheel Steering

The nosewheel steering system is a combination shimmy damper and dual mode steering system. It is electrically controlled by two switches on the stick grip and hydromechanically operated through inputs from the rudder pedals and flight control computers.

With the flight control computers operating, momentarily pressing the nosewheel steering button activates and engages nosewheel steering in the low mode (±16°) and NWS is displayed on the HUD. Holding the nosewheel steering button pressed selects the high mode (±75°) and NWS HI is displayed on the HUD. Momentarily pressing the autopilot disengage switch (paddle switch) disengages nosewheel steering until reengaged by the nosewheel steering button.

If the launch bar is extended, nosewheel steering is disengaged, however, the low mode may be engaged by pressing and holding the nosewheel steering button. On the ground, nosewheel steering is disengaged when power is removed from the aircraft. Nosewheel steering is also disengaged with weight off the nose gear. During landing, nosewheel steering is

An F/A-18D Hornet assigned to Marine All Weather Attack Squadron 224 (VMFA(AW)-224) 'Fighting Bengals' on a dynamic force employment mission in the US Central Command area of responsibility in May 2021. **US Air Force/TSgt Robert Harnden**

automatically engaged in the low mode with weight on the nose gear.

If the nosewheel steering system fails, it reverts to a free swivelling mode.

Brakes

The main landing gear wheels have full power brakes operated by toe action on the rudder pedals. An anti-skid system is combined with the normal system to prevent wheel skid. Normal brake pressure is supplied by HYD 2A. The anti-skid system modulates pilot demanded brakes to prevent tyre skid.

The anti-skid system is electrically controlled by a two-position switch on the lower left portion of the instrument panel.

A touchdown protection circuit prevents brake application on landing until wheel speed is over 50 knots, or if a wet runway delays wheel spin-up, three seconds after touchdown. A locked wheel protection circuit releases the brakes if the speed of one main wheel is 40% of the other main wheel. The locked wheel protection circuit is disabled at about 35 knots. The anti-skid system is totally disabled below 10 knots.

Normally limited by the anti-skid system, 3,000 psi hydraulic brake pressure is available and regulated only by pilot brake pedal forces. When using brakes at high speed without anti-skid protection, there is a very small margin between effective braking and blown tyres. Any force greater than approximately 55 to 60lb applied to the pedals (6° to 7° of pedal rotation) will likely result in blown tyres.

Emergency Brakes

The emergency brake system uses normal system brakes with independent hydraulic lines carrying emergency hydraulic pressure to the brake shuttle valve. The system is activated by pulling the emergency/parking brake handle out to the detent. The emergency brake system is powered by the HYD 2B system or the brake accumulator backed up by the APU accumulator.

When emergency brakes are selected, anti-skid is deactivated even if normal HYD 2A braking is available.

No warning/caution is displayed for emergency brake selection. The system is deactivated by pushing the emergency/parking brake handle back into the stowed position. The handle must be fully stowed (in both cockpits on the F/A-18B and F/A-18D variants) to ensure anti-skid is available.

Launch Bar

The launch bar is hydraulically extended and retracted by redundant springs. A locking tab mechanically locks the launch bar in the up position. A two position (EXTEND and RETRACT) launch bar switch on the lower left corner of the main instrument panel controls launch bar operation.

When the launch bar is fully extended it is held against the deck by deck-load control springs. The control springs allow vertical movement of the launch bar during taxi. As the aircraft is taxied into the launch gear, the launch bar drops over the shuttle and is held captive in the extended position as the shuttle is tensioned.

At the completion of the catapult stroke, launch bar/catapult separation occurs and the return springs cause launch bar retraction which allows the landing gear to be retracted. If the launch bar fails to retract after the aircraft is launched, nosewheel does not retract. A launch bar circuit breaker is on the left essential circuit breaker panel and when pulled deenergizes the launch bar electrical system.

Arresting Hook

The arresting hook system consists of a retract actuator/damper, fail safe manual latch and release, universal hook shank pivot and replaceable hook point. Hook control is a manual system which automatically extends the hook in case of a failure of the release system.

Hook extension is a free fall action assisted by a nitrogen charge in the actuator cylinder. Hook motion is dampened laterally by a liquid spring in the hook shank and vertically by the damper in the retract actuator cylinder which minimises hook bounce and provides hold down force for arresting cable engagement.

Without proper N_2 pre-charge (insufficient arresting hook snubber pressure), the arresting hook does not fully extend due to HYD 2 backpressure and air loads. If the arresting hook fails to extend because of this condition, shutting down the right engine reduces HYD 2 backpressure and allows sufficient extension (35° compared to 56° normal).

Wing Fold System

Each outer wing panel is folded upward to a vertical position by a wing fold mechanical/

F/A-18 HORNET

electrical drive. A wing fold unlock flag in the upper surface wing fold area provides a visual indication of the wing lock pins in the unlocked position. The wing lock control and wing fold/spread control are combined in the wing fold handle on the lower right main instrument panel. A wing safety switch is located so that a safety pin can be manually installed from the underside of the wing when absolute prevention of wing fold or spread is desired. The ailerons are locked in neutral when the wings are folded.

Cockpit Controls and Displays

The cockpit controls and displays which are used for navigation operation are on the multipurpose display group and on the upfront control (UFC).

The multipurpose display group consists of the right digital display indicator (DDI), the left DDI, the horizontal indicator (HI) on aircraft BuNo 161353 through BuNo 163782, the multipurpose colour display (MPCD) on aircraft BuNo 163985 and upward, the advanced multipurpose colour display (AMPCD) on aircraft BuNo 163985 and upward, the digital map set (DMS), the head-up display (HUD), the CRS (course) set switch, and the HDG (heading) set switch.

The multipurpose display group presents navigation, attack, and aircraft attitude displays to the pilot. The multipurpose display group converts information received from the mission computer system to symbology for display on the right and left DDIs, the HI/MPCD, and the HUD. The HUD camera records the outside world and HUD symbology. The left and right DDIs and the HI/MPCD contain pushbuttons for display selection and various equipment operating modes.

Digital Display Indicators

The right and left DDIs are physically and functionally interchangeable giving the ability to display desired information on either indicator or using either indicator to control the HUD or horizontal indicator displays. The left indicator is used primarily for stores status, built-in test status, engine monitor, caution, and advisory displays. The right indicator is normally used for radar and weapon video displays.

On aircraft BuNo 163985 and upward, the DDIs are NVG compatible and display three colours (red, yellow, and green) for stroke information. A monochrome version of the digital map can be selected on any of the DDIs. Either of the DDIs can provide raster generation for the HUD.

The HUD is on the centre main instrument panel. The HUD is used as the primary flight instruments, weapon status, and weapon delivery display for the aircraft under all selected conditions. The HUD receives attack, navigation, situation, and steering control information from the left or right DDI symbol generators (under mission computer control), and projects symbology on the combining glass for head-up viewing. The HUD is electrically interfaced with the UFC. On aircraft BuNo 163985 and upward the HUD has been enhanced by adding NVG compatible raster display capability to allow it to display video.

Entrance and Egress Systems

The cockpit area is enclosed by a clamshell type canopy. The main components of the canopy system are an electromechanical actuator which provides powered and manual operation of the canopy, and a cartridge actuated thruster with associated rocket motors for emergency jettison. Latching provisions consist of three latch hooks on the bottom of each side of the

In the winter of 1987, F/A-18A-equipped Marine Fighter Attack Squadron 122 (VMFA-122) 'Crusaders' deployed to Bardufoss Air Base, Norway for Exercise Cold Winter. This image shows a Hornet undergoing pre-flight checks on the snow laden flight line. **US Marine Corps/Cpl Gonzales**

F/A-18B Hornet BuNo 161707/03 in the unique white and orange livery of the US Naval Test Pilot School, retracts its landing gear on take-off from Naval Air Station Patuxent River, Maryland. **US Navy/PH2 Daniel Mclain**

An F/A-18C Hornet launches from the number three catapult aboard the aircraft carrier USS Dwight Eisenhower (CVN 69) underway in the Arabian Sea, on November 7, 2006. **US Navy/Lt Edward Ward**

canopy frame and two forward indexer pins on the lower leading edge of the canopy frame. When the canopy is closed, the latch hooks and indexer pins engage fittings along the canopy sill and the canopy actuator rotates the canopy actuation link over-centre, locking the canopy. A mechanical brake in the canopy actuator motor provides a redundant lock. An inflatable seal, installed around the edge of the canopy frame, retains cockpit pressure when the canopy is locked. A rain seal is installed outboard of the pressure seal to divert rainwater away from the cockpit. Windscreens installed on the F/A-18A, F/A-18B, F/A-18C and F/A-18D have been tested to determine their bird strike resistance.

Boarding Ladder
A boarding ladder, stowed under the leading-edge extension (LEX), provides access to the cockpit and upper aircraft area from the left side of the jet. Ladder extension and retraction can only be accomplished from outside the cockpit. To extend the ladder, the plane captain or pilot must manually support the ladder and release the forward and aft latches on the forward beam on the underside of the LEX, permitting the ladder to rotate down to the extended position. The drag brace locks when extended to its full length to provide longitudinal stability for the ladder. Lateral stability is provided for by the V-shaped side brace attached to the side of the fuselage. To stow the ladder, the plane captain or pilot must remove the rigid removable side brace connection from the fuselage. Pull the collar on the drag brace down permitting the telescoping drag brace to unlock and compress as the boarding ladder is rotated up and aft to the stowed position. The forward and aft latches are manually engaged and locked by pushing them full up until they are locked flush with the forward beam.

Ejection Seat
The various models of ejection seat are ballistic catapult/rocket systems that provide the pilot with a quick, safe, and positive means of escape from the aircraft.

The seat system includes an initiation system which, after jettisoning the canopy and positioning the occupant for ejection, fires the telescopic seat catapult. In the event of a canopy jettison failure during ejection, canopy breakers on the top of the seat give the capability for ejection through the canopy. As the seat departs the aircraft and the catapult reaches the end of its stroke a rocket motor on the bottom of the seat is fired. The thrust of the rocket motor sustains the thrust of the catapult to eject the seat to a height sufficient for parachute deployment even if ejection is initiated at zero speed, zero altitude in a substantially level attitude.

SJU-5 and SJU-6 Ejection Seat

Shortly after departing the aircraft a drogue gun is fired to deploy the drogue chute. The drogue chute either remains attached to the top of the seat or is released to deploy the main parachute, depending on altitude and the number of g applied on the seat. After a delay of 1.50 seconds, an automatic time release mechanism opens the main parachute container and releases the drogue chute to deploy the main parachute when conditions of altitude and g forces are met. The seat operates in three modes. At high altitude, the seat is allowed to freefall to below 14,500ft before the time release mechanism activates. At medium altitude, the time release mechanism actuates when the seat is below 13,000ft and above 7,500ft and acceleration forces are below 3g. At low altitude, below 7,500ft, g forces are not used as a condition for deploying the main parachute. The time release mechanism also releases the lap belts, inertia reel restraint straps, and leg restraint lines. Both the drogue gun and time release mechanism are actuated on ejection by trip rods attached to the aircraft structure.

The main parachute is a 17ft aero conical canopy type, stored along with the drogue chute(s) in a headbox container on top of the ejection seat. The parachute is steerable and contains water deflation pockets which aid in dumping air from the canopy after landing in water.

The seat contains controls for seat height adjustment, and for locking and unlocking the inertia reel shoulder restraint straps. A survival kit is installed in the seat pan.

SJU-17 Navy Aircrew Common Ejection Seat

Timing of all events after rocket motor initiation is controlled by the electronic sequencer which utilises altitude, acceleration, and airspeed information to automatically control drogue and parachute deployment, and seat/man separation throughout the ejection seat operational envelope. In the event of partial or total failure of the electronic sequence, a four second mechanical delay initiates a barostatic release unit which will free the occupant from the seat and deploy the parachute between 16,000 and 14,000ft if the ejection occurred in or above this altitude range. The emergency barostatic unit operates immediately after a four-second delay if the ejection occurred below 14,000ft. An emergency restraint release (manual override) system provides an additional back-up in the event of failure of the barostatic release unit. The seat is stabilised, and the forward speed retarded by a drogue chute that is attached to the top and bottom of the seat. The parachute deployment rocket is automatically fired to withdraw the parachute from its deployment bag. Full canopy inflation is inhibited until the g forces are sufficiently reduced to minimise opening shock. There are five modes of operation.

At high altitude the drogue chute deploys to decelerate and stabilise the seat. The seat falls drogue-retarded to 18,000ft where the drogue is released, the main parachute is deployed, and seat/man separation occurs. At medium altitude, between 18,000 and 8,000ft, and at low altitude below 8,000ft parachute deployment is automatically delayed from 0.45 to 2.90 seconds (depending upon airspeed and altitude after seat first motion) to allow the drogue chute to decelerate and stabilise the seat depending upon airspeed and altitude.

The main parachute is a 21ft aero conical canopy type, stored in a headbox container on top of the ejection seat. The parachute is steerable and contains water deflation pockets which aid in dumping air from the canopy after landing in water. The seat drogue chute is stored in a separate container on top of the drogue deployment catapult. The seat contains controls for adjusting seat height, and for locking and unlocking the inertia reel shoulder restraint straps. A survival kit is installed in the seat pan.

Two F/A-18A Hornet aircraft assigned to Strike Fighter Squadron 192 (VFA-192) 'Golden Dragons' during a mission flown from the aircraft carrier USS Midway (CV 41). US Navy/Lt Cdr Surbridge

Environmental Control System

The environmental control system (ECS) provides conditioned air to the cockpit and avionics. The ECS also provides cockpit pressurization, OBOGS source air, anti-g suit pressure, fuel tank pressurization, throttle boost, windshield anti-ice and rain removal, windshield defog, canopy seal, and waveguide pressurization. The ECS uses bleed air from the engines for operation.

Bleed Air System

Bleed air comes from the compressor section of each engine. A primary bleed air pressure regulator and shutoff valve is mounted on each engine and controls the flow of bleed air into the engine bay bleed air ducts. This valve can be manually commanded closed by the bleed air knob or is automatically commanded closed by the bleed air leak detection system, system overpressure sensor, or total loss of AC power.

The engine bay bleed air ducts are routed into the keel and are tied together. This common bleed air duct is routed through the secondary pressure regulator and shutoff valve which controls the flow of bleed air into the rest of the ECS. This valve can be manually commanded closed by the off position of the bleed air knob or is automatically commanded closed by the bleed air leak detection system or system overpressure sensor. The common bleed air duct is then routed from the keel across the top of the fuselage fuel tanks to the primary heat exchanger. For cross bleed engine starts, bleed air is routed to the air turbine starters through the isolation valve. A bleed air leak detection system which utilises temperature-sensing elements is installed. Elements are routed on each engine bay bleed air duct.

If a leak is detected in an engine bay bleed air duct, a single left or right bleed warning light is illuminated, the associated "Bleed Air Left/Right" voice alert is enunciated, and the associated primary bleed air pressure regulator and shutoff valve is commanded closed resulting in a single left or right bleed off caution.

Terrain Awareness Warning System

The terrain awareness warning system alerts the aircrew of a controlled flight into terrain (CFIT) condition during all mission phases. The system operates any time that the navigation mission computer (MC1) and TAMMAC digital mapping set (DMS) are functional. TAWS functions as a safety backup system and not as a performance aid. TAWS has been designed to eliminate false warnings, minimise nuisance warnings, and generate consistent aircrew response in all aircraft master modes. Five possible voice warnings are provided to indicate the correct initial response to an impending CFIT condition, and a visual cue is provided to indicate the recovery direction of pull, or in some instances, to command an increase in turn rate. All TAWS warnings should be treated as though an imminent flight into terrain condition exists. Pilot response to a TAWS warning should be instinctive and immediate.

TAWS uses data from the following inputs: air data computer, flight control computer, INS, radar altimeter, GPS, and digital terrain elevation data (DTED).

DTED resides in the DMS as part of the tactical aircraft moving map capability (TAMMAC) and is used to provide the forward-prediction capability that protects against flight into rising terrain.

When a DMS is not installed or is not operational, protection from CFIT events is provided by the Ground Proximity Warning System (GPWS). BIT may be initiated on the DMS by pressing the appropriate push tile of the BIT display. The BIT can take up to 185 seconds to complete. During the BIT, TAWS is not operational. Therefore, the GPWS algorithm is used to determine the presence of possible controlled flight into terrain events. There is no capability for pilot selection of GPWS if DMS is operational. The GPWS algorithm runs continuously with outputs being overwritten if TAWS is operational. This prevents erroneous values during an unexpected transition from TAWS to GPWS.

Ground Proximity Warning System

GPWS is a safety backup system that warns the aircrew of impending controlled flight into terrain (CFIT).

The GPWS is executed by an algorithm within the mission computer operational flight program software (OFP). It operates when MC1 is powered on. The GPWS option located on the aircraft sublevel display allows the pilot to disable/enable the system.

F/A-18 HORNET

An F/A-18A Hornet assigned to Strike Fighter Squadron 136 (VFA-136) 'Knighthawks' in February 1989. At the time the unit was based at Naval Air Station Cecil Field, Florida, assigned to Carrier Air Wing 7 and the USS Dwight D Eisenhower. The squadron started its first deployment in April 1989. **US Navy/Lt Cdr John Leenhouts**

Two-Seat Hornets
F/A-18B and F/A-18D aircraft (BuNo 161354 through BuNo 163778) have two cockpits in tandem configuration for performing the secondary trainer role without compromising the primary fighter/attack role. To make room for the aft cockpit, the fuel capacity in tank 1 is reduced to 316 gallons (2,150lb JP-5 or 2,050lb JP-4).

Using the front cockpit controls, the F/A-18B and F/A-18D avionics provide equivalent navigation and weapon system capabilities as those available in the single-seat F/A-18A and F/A-18C. The aft cockpit controls duplicate most front cockpit controls for navigation and weapon system control. However, weapons cannot be launched/released/fired from the aft cockpit.

F/A-18D: Night Attack
F/A-18D aircraft from BuNo 163986 upward are configured for the primary night attack role. The aft cockpit has the stick and throttles removed. The rudder pedals are fixed and disconnected from the rudder, brakes, and nosewheel steering. Two hand controllers are installed and the rear cockpit controls and displays operate independent of the front cockpit. Instruments and lighting are NVG compatible.

F/A-18D: Trainer
Night attack aircraft may be reconfigured to a trainer aircraft by removing the two hand controllers, adding throttles, stick, and connecting the rudder pedals. Aft cockpit controls and displays remain independent of the front cockpit.

F/A-18D: Reconnaissance
When retrofitted with reconnaissance equipment, an F/A-18D is designated as an F/A-18D(RC) (Reconnaissance Capable). It provides high-resolution, long-range standoff and overflight reconnaissance capabilities, day, or night, for all weather and under the weather missions. Electro-optical (EO), infrared (IR), and synthetic aperture radar (SAR) sensors gather image data. Image data is uploaded onto two onboard recorders and is available for downlink to ground stations for subsequent dissemination and exploitation. The aircraft is converted to RC configuration by installing the Advanced Tactical Reconnaissance System (ATARS) sensor suite into the nose bay in place of the 20mm gun. A data link pod can be loaded on the centreline to allow for the downlink of imagery data.

Canopy
The canopy system on the F/A-18B and F/A-18D is like the F/A-18A and F/A-18C aircraft except that an additional internal canopy jettison handle is installed in the aft cockpit. Note that the aft cockpit does not have an internal canopy switch or an internal manual canopy hand crank, and therefore, the canopy must be opened from the forward cockpit (or externally) unless it is jettisoned. To manually open the canopy using the internal manual hand crank, 224 counter clockwise manual crank turns are required. To manually open the canopy externally using a drive socket, 112 counter clockwise manual crank turns are required.

Ejection Seats
Ejection seats are installed in both cockpits. In addition, a sequencing system is installed to allow dual ejection initiated from either cockpit or single (aft) seat ejection initiated from the rear cockpit. A command selector valve is installed in the rear cockpit to control whether ejection from the rear cockpit is dual or single.

Digital Display Indicators
On aircraft BuNo 161354 through BuNo 163778, the corresponding left and right DDI in each cockpit presents the same information. The centre DDI displays the same information as the HI, except for the moving map display. Systems and presentations controlled by DDI/HI pushbuttons respond to the last action taken in either cockpit.

On aircraft BuNo 163986 and upward, the aft cockpit left and right DDI are independent of the front cockpit DDIs. However, the operation of both DDIs is identical to that of the front cockpit DDIs.

The aft cockpit of aircraft BuNo 163986 and upward also contain an MPCD/ AMPCD located between the left and right DDIs and are independent of the front cockpit MPCD/ AMPCD. However, MPCD/AMPCD operation is identical to that of the front cockpit MPCD/ AMPCD.

Head-Up Display
The aft cockpit does not contain a HUD, but HUD symbology can be selected for display from the menu on either the left or right DDI (on two-seat aircraft BuNo 161354 through BuNo 163778). This also selects HUD symbology on the same DDI in the front cockpit. On F/A-18D aircraft BuNo 163986 and upward, HUD symbology can appear on either DDI independent of the front cockpit. On the same group of F/A-18D aircraft, the HUD display is the only display not replaced by the SPIN recovery display when the SPIN recovery switch is actuated

The GPWS algorithm commands distinctive visual and aural cues to alert and direct recovery from an impending CFIT condition. All GPWS warnings should be treated as imminent flight into terrain unless reassessed situational awareness dictates otherwise. Pilot response to a valid warning should be instinctive and immediate, using the maximum capabilities of the aircraft to recover until safely clear of terrain.

Air Data Computer

The air data computer (ADC) is a solid-state digital computer which receives inputs from the angle-of-attack probes, total temperature probe, pitot static system, standby altimeter barometric setting, air refuelling probe position, magnetic azimuth system, mission computer, and landing gear handle position. Accurate air data and magnetic heading are computed. Computed data is supplied to the mission computer system, altitude reporting function of the IFF, engine controls, environmental control system, landing gear warning, and the fuel pressurization and vent system.

Angle-Of-Attack Probes

The left and right angle-of-attack (AOA) probes are the airstream direction sensing units. Case heaters are on whenever electric power is on the aircraft. Probe heaters are on when airborne. The approach and indexer lights operate from signals from the airstream detection sensing units. The AOA probe outputs go only to the ADC and each FCC. The outputs are electrically independent, not mechanically independent. The probes can be damaged in such a way that they freeze in position and continue to send signals to the ADC and FCCs.

Total Temperature Probe

The total temperature probe is mounted on the lower left fuselage aft of the nosewheel. The probe heater is on when airborne. The air data computer uses total temperature to calculate ambient temperature.

Joint Helmet Mounted Cueing System

The Joint Helmet Mounted Cueing System (JHMCS) allows the aircrew to target and employ existing short-range missiles (SRMs) and high off-boresight (HOBS) weapons, such as the AIM-9X Sidewinder, and cue the radar, FLIR, and other sensors. When using JHMCS to employ HOBS weapons, the aircrew can slave/acquire and shoot targets beyond the gimbal limits of the aircraft radar and designate ground targets. The main display provides a monocular 20° field of view that is visible in front of the pilot's right eye.

The main components of the JHMCS include the helmet mounted displays, electronics unit, HMD/AHMD off/brightness knobs, aft cockpit boresight reference unit, cockpit units, magnetic transmitter units, and seat position sensors in each cockpit. The JHMCS aircraft-integrated components can be flown with or without the helmet system.

Strike Fighter Squadron 127 (VFA-127) was an aggressor squadron based at Naval Air Station Fallon, Nevada between October 1, 1987, and its disestablishment on March 23, 1996. The unit was equipped with F/A-18A Hornets which were painted in this distinctive two-tone paint scheme for the aggressor role as seen in this shot at Fallon in June 1993. **US Navy/PH2 Bruce Trombecky**

Lon Nordeen and Mark Ayton provide an overview of the problems faced by the US Marine Corps to sustain its F/A-18 Hornet fleet through to final retirement in FY2030.

HORNET

US MARINE CORPS squadrons have been flying the F/A-18 Hornet strike fighter since 1982. First the Hornet replaced F-4 Phantoms in fighter, ground attack and reconnaissance roles. Later, two-seat F/A-18Ds replaced A-6E Intruders in reconnaissance, air control and all-weather strike missions.

The US Marine Corps has long been committed to operating a mix of conventional fixed-wing fighters, like the Hornet, and the V/STOL AV-8B Harrier II, for close air support from forward sites and amphibious assault ships. Today, the Corps is committed to operating a mix of fifth-generation F-35B STOVL and F-35C Carrier Variant Lightning IIs as replacements for fourth-generation F/A-18 Hornets and AV-8B Harrier IIs.

Because of the F-35's long and protracted development programme, combined with funding issues, fourth and fifth-generation Marine fighters will continue to operate together until 2030. The 2015 Marine Corps Aviation Plan called for accelerated retirement of the AV-8B fleet by 2025 and its replacement with F-35Bs. To fill the gap in the force, the Department of Defense, US Marine Corps and US Navy decided to extend the service life of F/A-18 Hornets until 2029 for active-duty units and 2030 for reserve units.

However, US Navy and US Marine Corps F/A-18 squadrons have been flying in combat for more than 25 years in Operation Desert Storm, Iraq No Fly Zone, Operation Enduring Freedom, Operation Iraqi Freedom, other military operations, and training. Intensity and the duration of combat operations have worn out most of the classic Hornet fleet. Sustained carrier operations of the US Marine Corps single-seat Hornets have also had a major impact on aircraft fatigue life.

Poor Shape

Years of high operational tempo have left the US Marine Corps Hornet fleet in poor shape and in need of deep maintenance. Funding issues and the condition of Hornet aircraft slowed the production output from US Navy Fleet Readiness Centers, where deep maintenance is performed.

During comments to the Seapower Subcommittee of the Senate Armed Services Committee back on April 20, 2016, Lieutenant General Jon Davis, then Deputy Commandant for Aviation, Headquarters, Marine Corps, said:

F/A-18C Hornets assigned to Marine Fighter Attack Squadron 112 (VMFA-112) 'Cowboys' alongside a KC-130J tanker assigned to Marine Aerial Refueler Transport Squadron 152 (VMGR-152) prior to aerial refuelling. **US Marine Corps/Sgt Booker Thomas**

PREPARING FOR RETIREMENT

"We have 87 aircraft that were mission capable. Out of those 87 airplanes, I put 30 airplanes in the training squadron and 40 airplanes deployed forward. There's not a lot left for the [remaining] units to train with. Priority goes to making sure every pilot is safe to fly." Davis added: "But there's very little time left for tactical proficiency."

Causes of the Shortfall

The shortfall occurred because the US Navy has converted all its classic Hornet strike fighter squadrons to the newer Super Hornet. By choice, the US Marine Corps elected to retain classic Hornets and AV-8B Harrier IIs and manage the risks of retaining such old aircraft until the service completes its F-35 transition - the service has programmes of record for 353 F-35Bs and 67 F-35Cs.

However, the US Marine Corps caught a cold with its F-35 transition because the F-35 programme took longer and cost far more to develop, assess and get into production than initially planned.

Keeping the Hornet fleet going, and at the same time upgrading the same jets to remain tactically viable for more than a decade, is a challenge.

US Marine Corps Hornet aircraft have been going through modification programmes to extend their service life for years.

Hornets built before Lot 17 (those with bureau numbers lower than 164945) go through a service life extension programme (SLEP) which replaces the aircraft's fuselage centre barrel, wing leading edges and includes other upgrades. Aircraft built in Lot 17 and higher go through a detailed inspection and repair programme with the goal of extending their service life and safety. Most major upgrades are completed at the aforementioned US Navy Fleet Readiness Centers.

During a Congressional Hearing back in 2014, Rear Admiral Michael Manazir, then US Navy Director of Air Warfare, reported on the surprises discovered on F/A-18 Hornet aircraft undergoing life extension. He said: "Corrosion impacts, I would say, caught us by surprise. When we opened aircraft up and saw the extent of the corrosion damage, we realised we couldn't just replace the parts we were going to replace. This made each aircraft coming into the depot kind of a one-off. We realised we couldn't just replace the parts — we also had

WWW.KEY.AERO 23

Marines perform an engine swap on an F/A-18C Hornet on the flight deck of USS Theodore Roosevelt (CVN 71). **US Navy/Mass Communication Specialist Seaman Chad Trudeau**

to look at the corrosion on the surrounding framework."

Manazir added: "We had not planned on operating the Hornet past 6,000 hours, so we did not do the normal corrosion control processes that were used on all-metal aircraft, like A-6 Intruders, A-7 Corsairs and F-14 Tomcats. We understood how corrosion affected metal. The science is different for corrosion of composites."

Defence cutbacks required by congressional sequestration reduced personnel and the flow of spare parts required for Hornet upgrades at the Fleet Readiness Centers, the implications from which are taking years to overcome.

Nothing New

Strike fighter shortfall in the Navy and Marine Corps is not a new issue. It was predicted for more than a decade and widely reported on. The US Congress has at times challenged some of the details (assumptions) provided by senior officers from the two services in hearings on the causes of the shortfall.

Back on March 26, 2015, during a FY2016 hearing of the House of Representatives Armed Services Committee, Representative Loretta Sanchez D-CA put some hard questions to Vice Admiral Paul Grosklags, Principal Military Deputy to the Assistant Secretary of the Navy (Research, Development, and Acquisition), Lieutenant General Jon Davis, Deputy Commandant of the Marine Corps for Aviation and Rear Admiral Michael Manazir, Director of the Air Warfare Division US Navy.

Rep. Sanchez: "Gentleman, I want to talk about the F-18. So, the navy, its testimony and information provided to this committee says by 2020 you will be short of 100 F-18s. And you also said that this number is due to grow because of particular factors. In looking back at the materials, we have had before this committee before, all the way back to 2009, we show a different shortfall every program year. For example, in 2009, the projection was 125 aircraft. A year later it was 145. In 2011 it was 177. In 2014 the shortfall was only 18 aircraft. So can you tell me the credibility when I see 18 to 100, that is a bit loose and a three, four, fivefold difference. Why is that, and what am I not seeing here? Do we just think that 82 planes will fall out of the sky this year? Why are the numbers so dramatically different? Are we guessing, do we really have ways in which we are trying to figure this out? And it appears to me the navy has a throughput problem, not a lack of aircraft, in terms of numbers. And as a result, should Congress be focusing on better

An F/A-18C Hornet, assigned to Marine Fighter Attack Squadron 323 (VMFA-323) 'Death Rattlers' launches from the flight deck of USS John C. Stennis (CVN 74). **US Navy/Photographer's Mate 3rd Class Ryan Restvedt**

An F/A-18A Hornet assigned to Marine Fighter Attack Squadron 115 (VMFA-115) in formation with the KC-130J tanker after aerial refuelling. *US Marine Corps/SSgt Kowshon Ye*

ONGOING US MARINE CORPS F/A-18 HORNET TO F-35 LIGHTNING TRANSITION PLAN

Marine Air Group 31, Marine Corps Air Station Beaufort

Current Hornet Squadron	F-35 Model	Scheduled transition period	Location
VMFA-115	F-35C	Q1-Q4 of FY2023	Beaufort to Cherry Point
VMFA(AW)-533	F-35B	Q1-Q4 of FY2024	Remains at Beaufort
VMFA-251	F-35C	Q1 FY2024 to Q1 FY2025	Beaufort to Cherry Point
VMFA(AW)-224	F-35B	Q1-Q4 of FY2025	Remains at Beaufort
VMFA-312	F-35B	Q1-Q4 of FY2027	Beaufort to Cherry Point

Marine Air Group 11, Marine Corps Air Station Miramar

VMFA-323	F/A-18C	Q1 FY2024 becomes FRD	Remains at Miramar
VNFA-323	F-35B	Q1-Q4 of FY2029	Remains at Miramar
VMFAT-101	F/A-18 Hornet FRS	Q1 FY2024 sundown	Remains at Miramar through to sundown
VMFA-232	F-35B	Q1-Q4 of FY2028	Remains at Miramar

US Marine Corps Forces Reserve

VMFA-112	F-35B	Q1-Q4 of FY2030	Ft Worth to Beaufort
VNFA-134	F-35B	From FY2030	Re-established at Miramar

funding the depot operations, rather than just buying more planes to put through the same rather inefficient depot repairs? What is going on here? What is the approach we need to be thinking about here?"

Sustainment Initiatives

The following six points provide details of the initiatives being undertaken by the US Navy and US Marine Corps in response to the questions posed by Sanchez.

First, more attention was focused on improving US Navy depot performance to overhaul F/A-18 Hornets so they could remain in service until replaced by F-35B and F-35C fighters.

Then Secretary of the Navy, Ray Mabus admitted in a March 1, 2016 Congressional report: "The near term challenge is managing a Department of Navy tactical aviation (TACAIR) force that has been reduced in capacity through a combination of flying many more flight hours than planned, pressurized sustainment and enabler accounts, legacy F/A-18 Hornet depot throughput falling short of the required output due to sequestration and other factors, and the impact of delays to completing development of the F-35 programme. As a result of aggressive efforts instituted in 2014 across the department to improve depot throughput and return more aircraft back to service, FY2015 depot throughput improved by 44% as compared to FY2014, returning to pre-sequestration levels. TACAIR aviation depots are expected to continue to improve productivity through 2017, and fully recover the backlog of F/A-18A-D aircraft in 2019."

Depot teams pulled parts from retired aircraft in storage with the 309th Aerospace Maintenance and Regeneration Group at Davis-Monthan Air Force Base, Arizona, ordered the manufacture of new parts and components and secured support from contractors.

Commenting on the situation in March 2017, Rear Admiral Mike Zarkowski, then Commander, Fleet Readiness Centers said: "The Naval Aviation Enterprise continues its efforts to reduce the number of aircraft in out-of-reporting [OOR] status due to depot-level maintenance through the implementation of critical chain project management at all the navy's Hornet Fleet Readiness Centers.

US Marines with Marine Fighter Attack Squadron 232 (VMFA-232) 'Red Devils' conduct pre-flight inspections on an AGM-88 High-Speed Anti-Radiation Missile at Andersen Air Force Base, Guam during August 2021. **US Marine Corps/LCpl Tyler Harmon**

US Marines with Marine Fighter Attack Squadron 232 (VMFA-232) 'Red Devils' load an AGM-88 High-Speed Anti-Radiation Missile onto an F/A-18D Hornet aircraft at Andersen Air Force Base, Guam. **US Marine Corps/LCpl Tyler Harmon**

An F/A-18A++ Hornet assigned to Marine Fighter Attack Squadron 115 (VMFA-115) 'Silver Eagles' with its aerial refuelling probe partly extended as the pilot prepares to refuel over Marine Corps Air Ground Combat Center, Twentynine Palms, California. The aircraft was participating in a large-scale, combined-arms training exercise intended to produce combat-ready forces capable of operating as an integrated Marine Air Ground Task Force. **US Marine Corps/SSgt Kowshon Ye**

A member of the airframes shop, assigned to Marine Fighter Attack Squadron 115 (VMFA-115) 'Silver Eagles' performs maintenance on the tail hook of an F/A-18A+ Hornet on the flight deck of USS Harry S. Truman (CVN 75). **US Navy/Photographer's Mate Airman Philip Morrill**

Additionally, we continue to leverage the industrial capacity offered by Boeing at Cecil Field [in Florida] and have further augmented our depot maintenance throughput by bringing on board L3 in Mirabelle, Canada, to help us through the peak demand for Hornet depot maintenance inductions."

Second, to help reduce the US Marine Corps aircraft shortfall, in 2014 the Naval Air Systems Command awarded contracts to Boeing and other suppliers to upgrade classic Hornets.

At the time, a spokesperson for the Deputy Commandant of the Marine Corps for Aviation told the author: "One of many levers the Naval Air Systems Command team is using to address the US Marine Corps F/A-18 shortfall and readiness issue is to initiate an upgrade plan for 30 Lot 10 and Lot 11 F/A-18C Hornets held in storage with the intent of updating them to a new F/A-18C+ standard. Aircraft held in storage are not the only ones getting upgraded. Factors used in determining which airframes to upgrade are the total number of flight hours and condition of the aircraft. This is identified to determine how much additional service time the US Marine Corps will get out of a particular aircraft once upgraded to ensure the best commitment of time and money."

Third, the US Navy and US Marine Corps had asked Congress for additional funding to reduce spare part shortages and improve maintenance issues. Both services received some additional support funds and the FY2018 budget called for US$8.6bn for flight operations, compared with US$7.5bn in FY2017. This increase equated to more than 100,000 flight hours across all models of the Hornet. Additionally, the FY2018 budget request increased funding for operations, maintenance, and spare parts to substantially higher levels than in previous years.

Fourth, the US Marine Corps instituted many changes in its Hornet squadron maintenance and support processes to reduce the number of aircraft not flying due to missing spare parts, support issues and damage.

Commenting, the deputy commandant's spokesperson said: "Aircraft readiness continues to slowly, but steadily, increase overtime. Recently, Headquarters Marine Corps Aviation began a Hornet independent readiness review, following completion of other independent readiness reviews on the H-1, CH-53E, AV-8B, and MV-22B, which were instrumental in the design of our readiness recovery strategy."

Fifth, Naval Air Systems Command developed and funded a plan to help ensure Hornets that remained in service were tactically viable.

And sixth, the Marine Corps tailored its F-35 transition plan, primarily by moving F/A-18 Hornet squadrons ahead of those operating the AV-8B taking advantage of the greater service life remaining in their Harriers.

Marine Corps Aviation Plan 2019

According to the F/A-18A-D Hornet (VMFA) plan listed in the most recent Marine Corps Aviation Plan published in 2019, the Hornet programme is focused on addressing inventory management, readiness degraders, solving chronic material shortfalls, and closing the mission capable (MC) gap.

High operational tempo, coupled with increased maintenance requirements at squadron level further degrades readiness and is a focus of F/A-18 programme initiatives.

A strategic aircraft by aircraft review of the

An F/A-18D Hornet assigned to Marine All Weather Attack Squadron 224 (VMFA-224) 'Fighting Bengals' approaches a basket extended from an aerial refuelling pod on a US Air Force KC-135 Stratotanker during a mission supporting Dynamic Force Employment over the U.S. Central Command area of responsibility in May 2021. **US Air Force/TSgt Robert Harnden**

A Marine applies sealant to an F/A-18C Hornet in the hangar bay aboard USS Theodore Roosevelt (CVN 71). **US Navy/Mass Communication Specialist 3rd Class Jennifer Case**

Marine maintainers install a new motor on a F/A-18D Hornet. **US Air Force/SSgt Westin Warburton**

An F/A-18 Hornet assigned to Marine Fighter Attack Squadron 112 (VMFA-112) 'Cowboys' taxis to the runway at Hyakuri Air Base, Japan, on December 9, 2021, during an operation in support of the aviation training relocation programme. **US Marine Corps/Cpl Evan Jones**

total active F/A-18 inventory is consistently being conducted by the Naval Aviation Enterprise.

As a result of US Navy F/A-18 Hornet divestment at the end of 2019, all US Marine Corps fleet squadrons were able to transition to aircraft built in Lot 15 and above with a similar configuration. The resultant increase in the US Marine Corps F/A-18 Hornet inventory has helped to further mitigate material shortfalls, and possible F/A-18C divestment by partner nations in the 2020 timeframe may provide additional opportunities to strengthen the Marine fleet of the type.

The F/A-18A-D team is engaged in inventory management, multiple readiness initiatives, planning an aggressive strike off charge/place in storage plan, and implementing re-engineered end of life planned maintenance interval (PMI) events. This review identifies 'best of breed' aircraft for the fleet and should aid the US Marine Corps' F/A-18 to F-35 transition plan through until 2030.

Part of this plan established a Level 3 flight line preservation facility at Marine Corps Aviation Station Miramar along with the resident Marine Aircraft Logistics Squadron 31 (MALS-31) being an aircraft custodian. This reduced the squadron level burden and concurrently provides flexibility and cost savings while effectively managing the Hornet inventory until its sundown.

US Marine Corp Aviation leadership is continuing to conduct executive level engagement with Department of Defense agencies supporting the F/A-18 Hornet, and with key vendors and original equipment manufacturers.

Participation in executive steering summit (ESS) enabled key readiness issues amongst the F/A-18 Hornet community is being addressed. Additionally, an independent readiness review identified further actions which, when taken increase supply responsiveness and increase mission capable rates.

Readiness is directly affected by the following supply and maintenance degradation aspects.
- The supply system is not able to keep pace with material demands.
- The quality of maintenance training curricula, maturation, and standardisation has not kept pace with readiness requirements.
- Current maintenance manning levels are unable to support demands for labour, a void filled with contract maintenance support.

The F/A-18 Hornet Service Life Management Program consists of the Center Barrel Replacement Plus (CBR+) and High Flight Hour (HFH) inspection programmes: CBR+ has extended the service life of numerous aircraft built in Lot 17 and below, and the HFH inspection has extended the life of the F/A-18 Hornet aircraft beyond 8,000 flight hours.

In parallel with CBR+ and HFH maintenance, the programme incorporates a combination of inspections, repairs, and several engineering change proposals to extend additional life of F/A-18A, F/A-18C and F/A-18D aircraft to 10,000 flight hours.

The Naval Aviation Enterprise has re-engineered the post-8,000-hour end of life maintenance plan. By developing a combined HFH/PMI-X depot event created significant savings of depot level maintenance man hours which is reallocated to SLEP MOD incorporation and other 'over and above' activities while simultaneously relieving the squadron level maintenance department of inspection requirements.

US Marine Corps' F/A-18 Hornet Final Fits

Avionics and Software Upgrades
Link-16 MIDS-JTRS four-channel radio (2018)
RNP/RNAV navigation systems enabling GPS approaches (2018)
Mode 5/Mode S IFF transponder (2019)
ADS-B (out) transponder (2020)
APG-79(V)4 AESA radar (2021)
On April 29, 2021, Raytheon Intelligence & Space delivered the first APG-79(V)4 radar prototype to Naval Air Systems Command for testing on an F/A-18 Hornet. The (V)4 is a version of the APG-79 (see p46) scaled to fit the forward fuselage of a legacy F/A-18 Hornet with an array comprising gallium nitride transmit/receive modules. The first production-standard set was due to be delivered in December 2021, one of 25 ordered in a US$83.6m production contract awarded in 2020.

Weapons Modernization
AIM-120D AMRAAM air-to-air missile (2016)
AIM-9X Block II air-to-air missile (2018)
AGR-20 APKWS rocket fitted with laser guidance kit (2018)

Digital Interoperability
AAQ-28 Litening Gen 4 pod-contained, multi-sensor laser target-designating, surveillance, and navigation system. Variable Message Format or VMF communications protocol used for transferring imagery for precise machine to machine targeting and real time mission assessment.

Increased Survivability
Automatic Ground Collision Avoidance System.
NAVWAR anti-jam antennas: NAVWAR is the official abbreviation of Air Navigation Warfare Program.
ALQ-214(V)5 IDECM upgrade (2018)
Details provided by the Harris Corporation, the manufacturer of the ALQ-214(V)4 and (V)5 systems, which are currently being installed on Super Hornet and Hornet aircraft respectively, say the system comprises a receiver, a modulator, a dual transmitter, a preamp, and a mini amp. The new variants use modular open system architecture compliant design, which enables re-programming to counter theatre specific configurations, and for future new components to be easily inserted. Operation is autonomous giving protection to the aircrew and aircraft against advanced radio frequency threats. Such threats are countered by the system with electronic countermeasure techniques that deny, disrupt, delay, and degrade launch and engagement sequences. Harris Corporation says each threat is identified, prioritised, countered, and displayed to the aircrew for situational awareness as well as self-protection.
ALR-67(V)3 radar warning receiver (2018)
ALR-67(V)5 digital radar warning receiver (Est 2023)
According to Raytheon, the ALR-67(V)3 uses channelised receiver architecture to enable detection of threat emitters in high pulse density, and interception of faint distant signals despite interference created by strong nearby transmitters. The digital measurement path of the receiver uses leading edge digital technology for improved reliability and low cost through reduced parts count, and improved performance through precision digital parameter measurements.
The ALR-67(V)5 is an all-digital, scalable variant.

Preparing for Retirement
Despite five operational F-35B squadrons (VMFA-121, VMFA-122, VMFA-211, VMFA-225 and VMFA-242) and one F-35C squadron (VMFA-314) now fully transitioned to the stealth fighter, the F/A-18 Hornet remains the US Marine Corps' most numerous and primary strike aircraft. According to the Marine Corps Aviation Plan 2019, F/A-18 Hornets support Marine Air-to-Ground Task Force commanders with arms coordination, multi-sensor imagery reconnaissance, and destroying surface targets and enemy aircraft, day, or night, under all weather conditions, during expeditionary, joint, or combined operations.

As part of its transition F-35 transition plan, US Marine Corps Aviation will start the drawdown of Marine Fighter Attack Training Squadron 101 (VMFAT-101) 'Sharpshooters', the F/A-18 training squadron, during FY2023, followed in Q1 FY2024 by VMFA-323's tasking with a Fleet Replacement Detachment to train Hornet aircrew until the type's retirement.

Marine Fighter Attack Squadron 112 (VMFA-112) 'Cowboys' based at Naval Air Station Joint Reserve Base Fort Worth, Texas is the US Marine Corps' operational reserve squadron and will support total force tactical aircraft (TACAIR) requirements until the squadron transitions to the F-35 in the FY2030 timeframe. At that time and per the TACAIR transition plan, VMFA-112 will relocate from Fort Worth, Texas to Marine Corps Air Station Beaufort, South Carolina.

A Marine maintainer performs maintenance on an F/A-18C Hornet in the hangar bay aboard USS Theodore Roosevelt (CVN 71) during a deployment in support of Operation Inherent Resolve. **US Navy/Mass Communication Specialist 3rd Class Taylor Jackson**

F/A-18 SUPER HORNET

Mark Ayton charts the development of the F/A-18 Super Hornet series of strike fighters.

ON JANUARY 11, 1988, McDonnell Douglas announced concept studies with the US Navy for an advanced version of the F/A-18 Hornet to be known as Hornet 2000. And on December 7, 1992, seven months after the Defense Acquisition Board approved initiation of the EMD, an engineering and manufacturing development contract was signed.

Super Hornet

The F/A-18E and F/A-18F Super Hornets are carrier-based strike fighter aircraft built by the McDonnell Douglas Corporation.

The multi-mission aircraft has an internal 20mm M61 gun/cannon, can carry AIM-7, AIM-9, and AIM-120 air-to-air missiles, and numerous air-to-ground weapons (see Missiles and Munitions pXX). The aircraft's fuel load can be increased with the addition of up to five external fuel tanks. The aircraft can be configured as an airborne tanker by carrying a centreline mounted air refuelling store.

The aircraft is designed with relaxed static stability to increase manoeuvrability and to reduce approach and landing speed. The aircraft is controlled by a digital fly-by-wire flight control system through hydraulically actuated flight control surfaces: ailerons, twin rudders, leading edge flaps, trailing edge flaps, leading edge spoilers (LEX), and differential stabilators. The leading edge of the wing incorporates a snag, which increases outboard wing area and increases roll authority in the approach and landing configuration. A speed brake function is provided by differential deflection of the primary flight control surfaces.

The pressurised cockpit is enclosed by an electrically operated clamshell canopy. An aircraft mounted auxiliary power unit (APU) provides self-contained start capability for the engines.

The two-seat F/A-18F is configured with tandem cockpits. The aft cockpit can be configured with a stick, throttles, and rudder pedals (the training configuration); or with two hand controllers, a UFCD adapter, and foot-operated communication switches (the missionised configuration). The aft cockpit controls and displays operate independently of those in the front cockpit.

Super Hornet was selected by the US Navy to provide a low-risk strike-fighter aircraft that could leverage the investment made in the F/A-18 Hornet and have capacity for growth utilising new technologies such as a

reduced RCS, integrated systems, and advanced countermeasures. The Super Hornet has limited commonality with the F/A-18 Hornet. The forward fuselage is based on the F/A-18C. New components include the wing, centre and aft fuselage, tail surfaces and engines. It has two notable design features, an enlarged strake to improve vortex lift in high angle-of-attack flight regimes and enlarged inlets for increased airflow. The inlet leading edges scatter radar waves and a fixed fanlike reflecting structure prevents microwave illumination off the engine fan blades. Both features are measures taken to reduce the aircraft's radar cross section which also include panel join serration.

A baseline Super Hornet has capacity for planned growth in avionics, software, flight-control, and mission computers.

Five of the weapon stations (centreline, inboard and mid-board) are fitted with fuel lines known as wet-stations. With a 480-gallon tank on each wet-station, a Super Hornet can carry 20,000lb. This enables an aircraft to carry sufficient 'give away' fuel for the tactical-tanking role. A Super Hornet carries an internal fuel load of 14,700lb, 36% more than the F/A-18C, which equates to a 40% extension of mission radius.

Engineering and Manufacturing Development Test Aircraft

Air Test and Evaluation Squadron 23 (VX-23) 'Salty Dogs' based at Naval Air Station Patuxent River in Maryland received five F/A-18E and two F/A-18F flight-test aircraft for the EMD programme. Each aircraft was instrumented when built for specific test missions in the EMD programme.

E1   F/A-18E BuNo 165164
Delivered: February 14, 1996
Test Missions: Flutter and Flying Qualities (FQ)

E1 completed the first supersonic test flights undertaken on the Super Hornet flight test program. It achieved Mach 1.1 on April 12, 1996, and Mach 1.52 April 13.
On February 21, 1997, F/A-18E1 flew with a with an aero servo elasticity stores configuration the first Super Hornet flight with weapons. The load comprised three 480-gallon fuel tanks, 2,000lb Mk84 bombs, two AIM-9 Sidewinders and high-speed anti-radiation missiles. At the time it was the highest take-off weight - 62,400lb - achieved by a Super Hornet.

The Super Hornet ITT began flutter flight-testing with F/A-18E1 in March 1996.

Flutter is vibration that continuously builds in intensity and does not damp out. Known as a destructive aero elastic phenomenon, flutter affects tails, wings, and stores.

Flutter is managed very carefully to make sure that whatever the airspeed, whatever the load condition - there is a predetermined airspeed margin reached before fluttering commences.

F/A-18E1 was flown in a clean (no external stores) configuration and 15 different external store configurations, at different speeds, and to different g-loads. Data collected verified the Super Hornet as safe from flutter throughout its flight envelope with no aero elastic limitations on carriage speeds of external stores. The aircraft

F/A-18F Super Hornet BuNo 168929/NA200 is the DCAG-bird with Strike Fighter Squadron 94 (VFA-94) 'Mighty Shrikes'. Armed with a single GBU-54 Laser Joint Direct Attack Munition, the aircraft is seen during a mission in support of Operation Inherent Resolve flown from the aircraft carrier *USS Nimitz* (CVN 68). **US Air Force/Senior Airman Duncan Bevan**

F/A-18 SUPER HORNET

completed flutter trials on October 23, 1998 and made its final flight on December 1, 2000.

On March 11, 1999, F/A-18E1 was used to refuel an F-14 Tomcat, an S-3B Viking and another Super Hornet, the first air-to-air refuelling made by a tanker-configured Super Hornet.

E1 was still with VX-23, held as a back-up aircraft for the EA-18G flutter flight-test programme being undertaken with F/A-18E22 BuNo 165779/SD101. The aircraft was retired to the museum at Patuxent River when the G-flutter programme was completed.

E2 F/A-18E BuNo 165165
Delivered: February 19,1996
Test Missions: Performance, Propulsion and FQ

E2 is currently used to assess antenna patterns as a static aircraft mounted on a plinth at the antenna farm at Naval Air Station Patuxent River.

E3 F/A-18E BuNo 165167
Delivered: February 1, 1997
Test missions: Loads, Ground loads, Noise and Vibration

F/A-18E3 was the seventh and final Super Hornet flight test aircraft delivered to VX-23 at Patuxent River. On February 26, 1997, E3 was loaded with three 480-gallon fuel tanks, two Mk84 bombs, two AIM-9 missiles and two AGM-88 High-speed Anti-Radiation Missiles and made a successful flight.

The aircraft is currently being used for the EA-18G flight-test programme. It completed parachute demonstration testing in 2005 and continues with ground and up and away load testing.

E4 F/A-18E BuNo 165168
Delivered: August 22, 1996
Test Missions: High Angle of Attack

E4 was the Super Hornet departure aircraft. It was painted in an orange and white colour scheme to give the aircraft high visibility for ground-tracking cameras. F/A-18E4 had a spin chute mounted on the aft fuselage between the tails for departure recovery during the flight-test programme. Aircraft E4 is now used as a maintenance trainer at Naval Air Station Oceana, Virginia.

E5 F/A-18E BuNo 165169
Delivered: October 25, 1996
Test Missions: Mission systems, Avionics and Weapon Separation

VX-23 undertook Weapon Separation for all load-outs carried by the Super Hornet. Not all the weapons in the Super Hornet arsenal were cleared during the EMD phase. VX-23 continues to drop weapons using aircraft E10. Since the EMD phase concluded, VX-23 has undertaken carriage of mixed loads on any stations comprising GBU-24s and JDAMs.

Weapon separation tests commenced on February 19, 1997, when a 480-gallon fuel tank was dropped by F/A-18E5 from 5,000ft completing the Super Hornet's first stores separation test.

Further separation tests were flown involving single, paired, multiple and ripple configurations from both the centreline and wing stations. By mid-May 1997, the Super Hornet Integrated Test Team had released ALE-47 flares, fired AIM-7 Sparrow, AIM-9 Sidewinder, AIM-120 AMRAAM, SLAM and Harpoon missiles, and dropped 500lb Mk82 and 1,000lb Mk83 bombs. The ALE-50 towed decoy had also successfully deployed from a Super Hornet.

Other missions included the first aerial refuelling with another Super Hornet in March 1999.

Aircraft E5 is now used as a maintenance trainer at Naval Air Station Oceana, Virginia.

F1 F/A-18F BuNo 165166
Delivered: May 21, 1996
Test Missions: Carrier suitability (CVS), ECS, FQ and Weapons testing

F1 was the first two-seat F/A-18F to be delivered to Naval Air Station Patuxent River. On August 5, 1996, F/A-18F1 completed the first three shots from a steam-powered catapult at the base and completed the programme's first arrested landing on August 21, 1996.

Five-months later, F1 completed initial sea trials aboard the USS *John C Stennis* (CVN 74). On January 18, 1997, Lieutenant Frank Morley landed F1 aboard the ship, the Super Hornet's

An F/A-18F Super Hornet assigned to Strike Fighter Squadron 122 (VFA-122) 'Eagles' shrouded in steam from the number one bow catapult on the *USS George H. W. Bush* (CVN 77) prior to launch. **US Navy/Mass Communication Specialist 3rd Class Brandon Roberson**

An F/A-18E Super Hornet assigned to Strike Fighter Squadron 151 (VFA-151) 'Vigilantes' over the ramp of the USS Abraham Lincoln (CVN 72). **US Navy/Mass Communication Specialist 3rd Class Michael Singley**

An F/A-18E Super Hornet assigned to Strike Fighter Squadron 113 (VFA-113) 'Stingers' launches off the flight deck of the aircraft carrier USS Carl Vinson (CVN 70) underway in the Indian Ocean during a bilateral training exercise with the Royal Australian Navy. **US Navy/Mass Communication Specialist Isaiah Goessl**

first carrier landing. During five days of tests, F1 performed 64 launches and arrested landings, and 54 touch-and-goes. The trials demonstrated a 10 knot slower final landing speed than the F/A-18C Hornet providing the pilot with better handling characteristics.

The aircraft was flown to Naval Air Station Lakehurst, New Jersey on February 25, 1998, to commence carrier suitability tests. Follow-on sea trials commenced aboard the USS *Harry S Truman* (CVN 75) on March 3, 1999 and during the night of March 8, F1 made the first night-time carrier launch and recovery by a Super Hornet.

Final sea trials conducted on USS *Harry S Truman* (CVN 75) that month included weapons carriage, stores separation, single-engine landings, crosswind take offs and landings, and automatic carrier landing system approaches.

During the Super Hornet EMD programme F1 also undertook ground loading tests. It undertook g-development during 2004 and is now based with Boeing at St Louis for special projects.

F2   F/A-18F BuNo 165170
Delivered: January 23, 1997
Test Missions: Mission systems and Weapon Separation

F/A-18F2 fired the first missile of the flight test programme, an AIM-9 Sidewinder on April 5, 1997. During EMD it conducted mission systems flight-test and Weapon Separation. It is wired for cameras used to capture the separation of bombs and missiles from the aircraft. F2 remains with VX-23.

During the three and a half year EMD programme, the seven flight-test aircraft assigned to VX-23 completed more than 15,000 test points, 3,172 flights and 4,673 flight hours to meet the EMD specification requirements. EMD concluded at Naval Air Station Patuxent River on April 30, 1999, on schedule and within the original programme set out in 1992.

F/A-18 SUPER HORNET

"To differentiate between an F/A-18 Hornet and an F/A-18 Super Hornet during flight deck operations, cats and traps, sailors gave the Rhino nickname to the Super Hornet."

Performance and Flying Qualities

VX-23 found one significant issue with the performance and flying qualities of the Super Hornet during the EMD programme. As the aircraft reached transonic speeds, it would roll off un-commanded when pulling g, an event known as wing-drop.

Wing-drop is an aerodynamic event caused by sub-standard wing camber design, which degrades tracking and handling the aircraft.

An initial fix comprised a porous door fitted over the wing-fold transmission, outboard of the wing. Over the long-term, the fix suffered long-term issues of corrosion and grease contamination.

After the EMD phase concluded a study known as TFQI (transonic flying qualities investigation) identified a more robust long-term fix.

Two changes were made to the wing. Solid doors known as a wing fence are fitted on top of the wing fold transmission and a slight filet is fitted in the wing snag. The changes resolved the wing-drop problem providing the same level of effectiveness as the porous doors.

Powerplant

The Super Hornet is powered by two General Electric F414-GE-400 low bypass, axial-flow, twin-spool turbofan engines each generating 22,000lb of thrust with afterburner.

The F414 evolved as an outgrowth of the original F404 Hornet engine originally known as the Growth II+ power plant which had been selected by General Electric and McDonnell Douglas for the proposed F/A-18 derivative originally known as Hornet 2000.

The Growth II+ engine was designated as the F414-GE-400 in 1991.

The F414 is the same size as the F404, a factor that minimised the number of structural design changes required to the aft fuselage of the Super Hornet. Engine architecture comprises a three-stage fan (low pressure compressor) and a seven-stage high pressure compressor and single-stage turbine that develops 22,000lb of thrust with afterburner, 4,300lb more than the F404.

The basic functions are supported by the engine driven accessory gearbox which drives the engine fuel pump, variable exhaust nozzle (VEN/start) fuel pump, lubrication and oil scavenge pump, engine fuel control, and alternator. Fuel flow from the VEN/start pump is used to drive the VEN actuator and to provide initial fuel pressure for main engine start.

An inlet device is installed in each engine intake to reduce the aircraft radar signature and to improve survivability.

The additional performance given by the F414 is generated by the engine's new design and use of new technology.

General Electric Aircraft Engines received an engineering and manufacturing development (EMD) contract in May 1992 covering development and delivery of 12 factory and 21 flight test engines. The first F414 engine test occurred on May 30, 1993. The EMD contract involved 12,685 hours of engine and major component tests including 5,700 hours of accelerated simulated mission endurance testing (ASMET) - tests that accumulate defined operational flight cycles in a test cell quicker than using an aircraft.

Thirteen factory test-engines were built and ground-tested at the General Electric

Flight deck personnel watch on as an F/A-18F Super Hornet assigned to the 'Black Knights' of Strike Fighter Squadron 154 (VFA-154) from a waist catapult of the aircraft carrier *USS John C. Stennis* (CVN 74), when underway in the Persian Gulf. **US Navy/Mass Communication Specialist 2nd Class Ron Reeves**

Aircraft Engine plants at Lynn, Massachusetts and Peebles, Ohio. Survivability testing was undertaken at NAWS China Lake, California while gyro, acoustics and infra-red signature testing took place at Naval Air Station Lakehurst, New Jersey.

After six and a half years in EMD and 12 major revisions of the engine test plan, the F414 successfully completed its Limited Production Qualification (a 1,050-hour ASMET) and Preliminary Flight Qualification (a 300-hour running at 'redline' ASMET) milestones and the first production engine was delivered on schedule in July 1998.

Engine Components

The F414 fan provides 16% more airflow than the F404 fan with improved bird strike and foreign object damage-resistance characteristics. A tandem blisk (integral blades and disks) is used in the second and third stages. Blisk construction improves durability by eliminating life-limiting dovetail joints between each blade, reduces weight and increases performance.

The engine core comprises a compressor, combustor, and high-pressure turbine. The F414 compressor is a seven-stage design; the first three rotor stages are blisk construction yielding a 5% higher airflow than the F404 engine.

The F414 combustor has an annular (outer and inner shell) design with a myriad of 30,000 laser-drilled holes to tailor the cooling flow through the combustor shelves. This provides control and even temperature distribution coming out of the combustor minimising the impact on the turbine blades immediately behind the combustor.

The F414 turbines feature mono crystal blades and thermal barrier coated air foils. The materials help to extend the life of the components from the high temperature environment. F414 turbines have boltless retainer construction eliminating life limiting boltholes and disks to improve durability and overall maintenance life cycle costs. The turbines use thermally matched stator/rotor to help minimise droop and improve overall performance.

The afterburner has an air-cooled radial segmented flame holder system comprising several individual segments bolted to the inside of the combustor casing. Cooler air passing through the fan is ducted between the outer combustion case and the liner inside it keeping it cool. The cool air is at a higher pressure than the exhaust gas inside the afterburner. Some of the cool air passes through the individual segments of the flame holder maintaining a relatively constant temperature. Spray bars inside the flame holders apply the fuel.

In older engine designs the mix of the afterburner's high temperature with the cold temperature of the fuel caused thermal quenching during each engine cycle. That caused cracking and a need for maintenance.

The F414 engine has a variable exhaust nozzle (VEN), to optimise performance. A set of flaps in the VEN slide across each other as the nozzle opens and closes to maintain the flow path. Durability is achieved in the very high temperature environment by using ceramic matrix composite material. Matrix refers to the composite fibres that provide the strength to withstand the temperature and forces on the unit.

The aircraft does not have a cable throttle. It uses a fly-by-wire throttle sending signals

Strike Fighter Squadron 192's CAG-bird F/A-18E BuNo 169736/NE300 launches from the number four waist catapult of the aircraft carrier *USS George Washington* (CVN 73). **US Navy/Mass Communication Specialist Clemente Lynch**

Sailors transport a GE F414 jet engine in the hangar bay of the *USS Carl Vinson* (CVN 70). **US Navy/Mass Communication Specialist 3rd Class Erin Zorich**

Sailors aboard the *USS Carl Vinson* (CVN 70) move an F414 jet engine while conducting aircraft maintenance in the hangar bay. **US Navy/Mass Communication Specialist 3rd Class Erin Zorich**

to a dual channel FADEC (full-authority, digital electronic control) to request the required power level and FADEC responds appropriately. The system controls fan and compressor variable geometry, VEN actuators and fuel schedules for main and augmenter combustion. FADEC is also integrated with the aircraft control system to perform special functions such as Reduced Authority Thrust System when landing using limited carrier arresting cable loadings.

Dual channel means FADEC uses two separate computers in the one box. The architecture is an active/standby configuration where one channel is in control with the other in a standby mode ready to automatically assume full control should a failure of the active channel occur. Each time the engines are started, the opposite channel to the previous engine start takes command.

FADEC also functions as an integrated part of the aircraft system providing troubleshooting, fault detection and isolation capabilities down to component level.

Depending on the level of fault or degradation some engine fault codes are notified to the pilot others go straight to the wheel well screen and are displayed in MSP format via the MIL-STD-1553 data bus.

An F414 engine comprises six interchangeable modules: Fan, Compressor, Combustor, High Pressure Turbine, Low Pressure Turbine and Afterburner with bottom-mounted accessories.

Each engine is interchangeable between the left and right engine chamber and can be changed in under 30-minutes.

Reliability centred maintenance requires an inspection every 2,200 operating hours with no scheduled overhauls. The F414 has eight bore scope inspection ports and an In-flight Engine Condition Monitoring System (IECMS).

Flight Testing
The first flight of a Super Hornet powered by two F414 engines took place on November 29, 1995, at Boeing's plant at Lambert Field in St. Louis, Missouri. Flight-testing commenced at Naval Air Station Patuxent River, the primary test site, two months later in January 1996. Initial sea trials commenced in February 1997 aboard the USS *John C Stennis* (CVN 74) and follow-on sea trials in early March 1999 aboard the USS *Harry S Truman* (CVN 75). During 12-days of sea trials the two participating F/A-18F Super Hornets logged 140 catapults and recoveries, 11 bolters, 47 wave-offs and 188 touch and goes — with zero engine squawks. Flight-testing on 21 different engines accumulated 18,480 engine flight hours over the four years between maiden flight and OPEVAL.

By February 2007, General Electric had delivered over 700 F414-GE-400 engines to the US Navy fleet, which had accumulated over 700,000 cumulative engine flight hours.

Fuel System
A Super Hornet is fitted with four internal fuselage tanks (tanks 1 through 4), two internal wing tanks (left and right), two fuselage vent tanks, and two vertical vent tanks. Tanks 2 and 3 are engine feed tanks while tanks 1, 4, and the wing tanks are transfer tanks. Total fuel can be increased by the carriage of up to four 480-gallon external fuel tanks on the centreline, inboard, and mid-board pylons. The aircraft can also be configured as an airborne tanker with the carriage of a centreline mounted air refuelling store (see pXX).

The aircraft's fuel system comprises the following subsystems: engine feed, motive flow, fuel transfer, tank pressurisation and vent, thermal management, refuelling, fuel dump, fuel quantity indicating, and fuel low level indicating.

Refuelling System
The aircraft can be refuelled on the carrier flight deck through a single point refuelling receptacle or inflight through a hydraulically actuated inflight refuelling probe. The receptacle is located behind door 8R on the forward right fuselage while the probe is located on the upper right side of the fuselage forward of the windscreen. A fuel pressure regulator/surge suppressor is installed downstream of the refuelling probe to control pressure spikes associated with aerial refuelling. Fuel from the single point receptacle or the refuelling probe enters the refuel/defuel line and is routed to all internal and external tanks.

Secondary Power System
The aircraft's secondary power system contains two airframe mounted accessory drives (AMAD) and a single auxiliary power unit (APU).

The APU is a small gas turbine engine used to generate a source of air used to power the ATS for normal engine start or to provide an alternate air source for the environmental control system (ECS). The APU is located between the engines, with intake and exhaust facing downwards.

The aircraft battery provides electrical power for APU ignition and start. A hydraulic motor powered by the APU accumulator is used to start the APU. The APU receives fuel from the left engine feed line upstream of the left engine feed shutoff valve. During normal operation, the APU shaft turns a separate compressor which supplies air for main engine start or alternate ECS operation.

Electrical Power Supply System
The electrical power supply system consists of two generators, two transformer-rectifiers (TR), one battery with dedicated battery charger, and a power distribution (bus) system.

Each generator provides a primary AC source and three isolated DC sources from a permanent magnet generator (PMG). During normal operation, the left generator powers only the left buses while the right generator powers only the right buses. If one generator fails, the other generator can carry the entire electrical load of the aircraft. Battery power is provided for normal engine start. External electrical power can be applied to power the entire system when on the ground.

Sailors prepare to launch an F/A-18E Super Hornet on the flight deck of the aircraft carrier *USS Dwight D. Eisenhower* (CVN 69), in the Mediterranean Sea. **US Navy/Mass Communication Specialist 3rd Class Cameron Pinske**

F/A-18 SUPER HORNET

Hydraulic Power Supply System
The hydraulic power supply system is a dual pressure system (3,000 and 5,000psi). The aircraft uses hydraulic power to actuate primary flight control surfaces and to run the following utility hydraulic functions: landing gear, wheel brakes and anti-skid, hook, launch bar, refuelling probe, nosewheel steering (NWS), gun, and parking brake. Two hydraulic accumulators provide emergency hydraulic power for critical utility functions.

Hydraulic System
The hydraulic power supply system incorporates two independent hydraulic systems, HYD 1 and HYD 2. Each hydraulic system is divided into two branches providing four independent hydraulic circuits identified as 1A and 1B for the left system and 2A and 2B for the right system. HYD 1 circuits are dedicated solely to flight controls. HYD 2A powers both flight controls and most utility hydraulic functions. HYD 2B powers the flight controls and arresting hook and pressurises both the APU and emergency brake accumulators.

All flight control surface actuators are powered by one HYD 1 circuit and one HYD 2 circuit, either simultaneously or through hydraulic switching valves.

The utility system operates at 3,000psi only. Two pressure reducers, one on HYD 2A and one on HYD 2B reduce utility circuit pressure to 3,000psi when pump output is 5,000psi.

Utility Hydraulic Functions
The utility hydraulic functions are powered by HYD 2 and include landing gear extension and retraction, nosewheel steering, wheel braking and anti-skid, launch bar extension, arresting hook retraction, and in-flight refuelling probe extension and retraction.

Landing Gear System
The landing gear is a tricycle design and includes a nose landing gear with steerable nosewheel and two fixed main landing gear. The nose landing gear retracts forward, while the main landing gear retract aft and inwards. When the landing gear is extended, all landing gear doors remain open.

Planing Links
Each main landing gear assembly incorporates a planing link, which is designed to properly align the main wheels after landing gear extension. The joint which connects the wheel to the main landing gear lever is designed to rotate off-axis, so that the wheel fits properly into the main landing gear wheel well. The planing link rotates the main wheel from its stowed orientation, aligns it with the longitudinal axis of the aircraft, and locks over-centre. A planing link proximity switch is used to verify proper planing link position and thereby proper wheel alignment.

Normal Landing Gear Extension and Retraction
Normal landing gear extension and retraction is electrically controlled by the landing gear handle and uses hydraulic pressure from HYD 2A. With weight off the nose gear and the launch bar retracted, moving the landing gear handle to the up position sends an electrical signal to the landing gear selector valves to initiate normal landing gear retraction. Likewise, moving the LDG GEAR handle to the DN position sends an electrical signal to the landing gear selector valves to initiate normal landing gear extension.

Nosewheel Steering System
The nosewheel steering system (NWS) is used to provide directional control and shimmy damping during ground operations. The NWS hydraulic power unit, attached to the nose landing gear strut, is electrically controlled by commands from the flight control computers and is hydraulically actuated by pressure from HYD 2A (primary) or HYD 2B/APU accumulator (backup). In the event of a HYD 2A failure, a pressure-biased shuttle valve routes HYD 2B pressure (if available), or APU accumulator pressure to the NWS unit for backup operation.

Wheel Brake System
The aircraft's wheel brake system provides normal braking, anti-skid, emergency braking, a parking brake, and main wheel anti-spin. Normal braking uses HYD 2A pressure and is capable of functioning with a separate anti-skid system. The anti-skid system, when enabled, provides maximum braking effectiveness on wet runways or during heavy braking by preventing wheel skid. When selected, emergency braking uses HYD 2B pressure, if available, or brake and APU accumulator pressure to provide backup braking capability following a HYD 2A failure. The anti-spin function stops main landing gear wheel rotation prior to landing gear retraction.

An F/A-18E Super Hornet assigned to Strike Fighter Squadron 143 (VFA-143) 'Pukin' Dogs' launches from the number three waist catapult of the *USS Abraham Lincoln* (CVN 72). **US Navy/Mass Communication Specialist 3rd Class Michael Singley**

Wheel Brake Assembly

Each main landing gear wheel is fitted with hydraulically actuated multiple disk brakes. There are two independent sets of brake lines running to each wheel brake assembly: the normal brake line pressurised by HYD 2A and the emergency brake line pressurised by HYD 2B or the brake and APU accumulators. Only one set of brake lines can be pressurised at any given time. A shuttle valve on each wheel brake assembly switches from normal to emergency brake pressure, depending on which is applied.

Each wheel assembly incorporates a fuse plug which is designed to melt and deflate the tyre at temperatures below those which would result in a catastrophic tyre blowout.

Anti-skid System

The anti-skid system performs four basic functions which are designed to maximise braking effectiveness during landing rollout: touchdown protection, wheel spin-up override, skid control, and locked wheel protection.

Launch Bar System

The launch bar is electrically controlled, hydraulically extended, and mechanically retracted. With weight on the nose gear, placing the launch bar switch to extend energises the launch bar control valve and routes HYD 2A pressure to unlock, lower, and hold down the launch bar.

With the launch bar extended, returning the launch bar switch to retract de-energises the launch bar control valve, isolates HYD 2A pressure, and allows dual retract springs to mechanically return the launch bar to the up and locked position. A launch bar proximity switch is energised when the launch bar is fully retracted.

When the launch bar is fully extended it is held against the deck by HYD 2A pressure. Deck load springs allow vertical movement of the launch bar during taxi over the catapult shuttle. When the aircraft is placed in tension on the catapult, the launch bar is held captive in the extended position by the shuttle. Once in tension, the launch bar switch should be placed to retract to remove HYD 2A pressure from the launch bar.

At the end of the catapult stroke, launch bar/shuttle separation occurs and allows the retract springs to return the launch bar to the up and locked position. When engaged, the launch bar uplock prevents the launch bar from dropping to the deck due to g-loads during landing.

If the launch bar does not return to the up and locked position after catapult launch (launch bar proximity switch not energised), the nose landing gear cannot be retracted. In this case, placing the landing gear handle up will raise the main landing gear and leave the nose landing gear extended.

Arresting Hook System

The arresting hook is always down-loaded by a nitrogen-charged accumulator (arresting hook snubber) contained in the arresting hook retract actuator. Arresting hook extension is therefore accomplished by mechanically releasing the arresting hook uplatch mechanism (hook handle down) and allowing snubber pressure and gravity to extend the hook. The hook should extend in less than two seconds. At touchdown, the arresting hook snubber controls hook bounce and provides a hold down force for arresting cable engagement.

Arresting hook retraction is accomplished by raising the hook handle. This electrically opens the aft isolation valve and the arresting hook selector valve, routing HYD 2B pressure to the arresting hook retract actuator. HYD 2B pressure overcomes the snubber down-load pressure and raises the hook. The arresting hook uplatch mechanism captures and locks the hook in the up position. The hook should retract in less than four seconds. If HYD 2B pressure is lost, the arresting hook cannot be retracted.

Wing Fold System

The aircraft's outer wing panels are designed to fold vertically to reduce the amount of deck space occupied by the aircraft in the carrier environment. Each wing contains an independent wing fold mechanism, which consists of two electric motors (one to lock/unlock the wings and one to spread/fold the wings). During normal operation, the wings are spread, locked, unlocked, and folded in unison.

Wing Fold Mechanism

Each wing fold mechanism contains a DC electric motor, which locks and unlocks the wings, and an AC electric drive unit, which

spreads and folds the wings. When the wings are spread and locked, a locking bolt is electrically driven through the wing fold hinge, holding it in place. When the wings are unlocked, a wing unlock flag (commonly called a beer can) protrudes from the upper surface of the wing near the leading edge of the wing fold hinge, indicating that the locking bolt is unstowed. The shaft of each beer can is painted red for easy identification. When the wings are locked, the top of the beer can should be flush or near flush with the upper surface of the wing, and no red should be showing.

Additionally, when the wings are folded, the ailerons are mechanically locked in the faired position by a hook on the inboard aileron hinge, which engages an aileron locking pin. The aileron locking pin is mechanically extended as the wings fold. The hook and locking pin are designed to prevent the ailerons from blowing inboard over the trailing edge flap when hydraulic power is not applied. If an aileron locking pin should break, it is possible for the aileron to blow inward over the trailing edge flap. If this condition exists during engine start, the trailing edge flap will retract into the aileron, damaging both surfaces.

Each wing fold mechanism also contains a wing safety switch, which electrically prevents wing fold movement. The safety switch is activated by a 'remove before flight' pin inserted in the underside of the wing near the wing fold hinge.

For ground crew operations (such as loading missiles on the wingtip rails), each wing can be manually unlocked, folded, or spread. The beer cans can be manually extended by inserting a screwdriver into the wing unlock motor (underside, leading edge). Once unlocked, the wings can be folded or spread by inserting a speed handle into the electric drive unit located on the underside, trailing edge.

Wing Fold Operation

With the wings folded, wing spread, and lock are commanded by placing the wing fold switch to spread. The spread command is sent directly to the electric drive units to spread the wings. When each wing reaches the completely spread position, power is removed to that electric drive unit, and that wing is automatically commanded to lock.

Once the wings are spread and locked, the ailerons will droop to the position scheduled by the flight control computers based on the flap switch position.

Flight Control System

The flight control system (FCS) is a fly-by-wire, full authority control augmentation system (CAS). The FCS provides four basic functions: aircraft stability, aircraft control, departure resistance, and structural loads management.

An F/A-18E Super Hornet assigned to Strike Fighter Squadron 81 (VFA-81) 'Sunliners' launches from the USS Harry S. Truman (CVN 75). **US Navy/Mass Communication Specialist 3rd Class Rebekah Watkins**

An F/A-18E Super Hornet assigned to Strike Fighter Squadron 115 (VFA-115) 'Eagles' launches from the flight deck of the USS Nimitz (CVN 68) underway off the coast of Southern California. **US Navy/Mass Communication Specialist 2nd Class Shannon Renfroe**

An F/A-18E Super Hornet assigned to Strike Fighter Squadron 143 (VFA-143) 'Pukin' Dogs' launches from the flight deck of the aircraft carrier USS Dwight D. Eisenhower (CVN 69). The aircraft is loaded with an aerial refuelling store on the centreline and four external 480-gallon tanks. **US Navy/Mass Communication Specialist Seaman David Danals**

An F/A-18E Super Hornet assigned to Strike Fighter Squadron 151 (VFA-151) 'Vigilantes' immediately ahead of launch from the number four waist catapult of the aircraft carrier USS Abraham Lincoln (CVN 72). **US Navy/Photographer's Mate 3rd Class Jordon Beesley**

Since the basic airframe is statically neutral to slightly unstable, a primary function of the FCS is to maintain aircraft stability at all flight conditions. The FCS also provides full authority control of the aircraft by implementing the basic flight control laws which determine aircraft response to pilot inputs.

Pilot inputs from the stick and rudder pedals send electrical commands to two quad-redundant, digital flight control computers (FCC A and FCC B). There is no mechanical linkage between the stick and rudder pedals and the flight control surfaces. FCC software determines what commands are sent to the various flight control surfaces to exercise pitch, roll, and yaw control of the aircraft. Additionally, the FCS provides departure resistance by either refusing to accept or by tailoring pilot inputs that would otherwise lead to an aircraft departure. Lastly, the FCS provides structural loads management by limiting g-available to prevent an aircraft overstress or by retracting flight control surfaces at airspeeds that would otherwise exceed the structural limits of the airframe.

Flight Control Surfaces

The aircraft has 12 primary flight control surfaces including leading edge flaps (LEFs), trailing edge flaps (TEFs), ailerons, twin rudders, horizontal stabilators, and spoilers. LEFs, TEFs, ailerons, and stabilators can be moved both symmetrically or differentially for pitch and roll control.

Pitch control is accomplished with symmetric stabilators and, in some conditions, with rudder toe-in or rudder flare. Roll control is accomplished with combinations of ailerons, differential stabilators, differential LEFs, and differential TEFs dependent on flight condition and CAS operating mode. The twin rudders deflect symmetrically for directional control. There is no dedicated speed brake surface. Instead, a 'speed brake function' is provided by partial deflection of several of the primary flight control surfaces.

Hydraulic power to all flight control surface actuators is supplied by HYD 1 and HYD 2. Stabilator and trailing edge flap actuators are powered simultaneously by one HYD circuit from each system. All other actuators are powered by a single primary HYD circuit, with backup hydraulic power available through a hydro-mechanical switching valve.

Spoilers

The spoilers are mounted on top of the fuselage near the aft end of the LEX. The spoilers are controlled by the FCCs and have two fixed positions: 0° (down) or 60° trailing edge up.

Flight Control Computers

Two flight control computers (FCC A and FCC B) provide the computations which

F/A-18 SUPER HORNET

implement the aircraft's flight control laws. A four-channel architecture is used to provide FCS redundancy. Each FCC contains two individual central processing units (CPUs), which each run one channel of the FCS: channels 1 and 2 are resident in FCC A, with channels 3 and 4 in FCC B.

Each of the four CPUs runs independent and parallel flight control computations. Sensor inputs as well as CPU outputs are continuously monitored by the FCCs for agreement. When there is disagreement, the erroneous signal is discarded, if possible. The automatic flight control system or autopilot provides three basic functions: pilot relief, coupled steering, and data link control.

Weapon Systems Controls

All the primary controls for the aircraft's weapon systems (weapons, sensors, and displays) are located on the front cockpit throttles and stick, the rear cockpit throttles, and stick (on an F/A-18F in trainer configuration), or the rear cockpit hand controllers (on an F/A-18F in missionized configuration). The hands-on throttles and stick concept, allows the aircrew to manipulate the weapon systems without removing their hands from the aircraft's primary flight controls.

Environmental Control System

The environmental control system (ECS) uses engine bleed air to provide pressurisation, heating, and cooling air to various aircraft systems. Warm air is provided for internal fuel tank pressurisation (Lot 23 aircraft and below), external fuel tank pressurisation, canopy seal inflation, g-suit operation, radar waveguide pressurisation, windshield anti-ice and rain removal, gun gas purge, recce bay heating, and on-board oxygen generating system operation. Cold, dry conditioned air is provided for avionics cooling. Warm and cold air are mixed to provide temperature-controlled air for cabin heating, cooling, and pressurisation and windshield defog.

A liquid cooling system (LCS) is used to cool the radar transmitter. A digital ECS controller is used to schedule ECS output, regulate system temperatures, monitor system health, and detect and isolate faults.

Canopy System

The cockpit is enclosed by a clamshell type canopy. The main components of the canopy system are an electromechanical actuator, which provides powered and manual operation, and a cartridge actuated thruster with associated rocket motors, which provides emergency jettison. When closed, the canopy is latched in place by three hooks on the bottom of each side of the canopy frame and two forward indexer pins on the lower leading edge of the canopy frame. When the canopy is closed, the latch hooks and indexer pins engage fittings along the canopy sill, and the canopy actuator rotates the canopy actuation link over-centre, locking the canopy. A mechanical brake in the canopy actuator motor provides a redundant lock. An inflatable seal, installed around the edge of the canopy frame, retains cockpit pressure when the canopy is locked. A rain seal is installed outboard of the pressure seal to divert rainwater away from the cockpit.

Boarding Ladder

A five-step boarding ladder, stowed under the left LEX, provides access to the cockpit and the top of the aircraft. Ladder extension and retraction can be accomplished only from outside the cockpit, either manually or by the ladder remote release button.

The ladder is extended manually by releasing the latch on the stow assist handle on the ladder's left rail (allowing it to drop slightly) and while supporting the ladder, rotating the stow assist handle to vertical (releasing the remaining two mechanical uplocks on the underside of the LEX). The ladder rotates down to the extended position. The stow assist handle is then secured. The drag brace locks when extended to its full length to provide longitudinal stability for the ladder. Lateral stability is provided by a V-shaped side brace attached to the side of the fuselage.

Normal cockpit egress is accomplished by grasping the canopy sill firmly with both hands, leaning outboard and, using the ladder marking decals as a guide, stepping over the LEX toward the ladder. The first step is approximately 15 inches below the leading edge of the LEX.

The ladder is stowed by detaching the rigid side brace connection from the fuselage. Pulling the collar on the drag brace down permits the telescoping drag brace to unlock and compress as the boarding ladder is rotated up and aft to the stowed position. The latches are manually engaged and locked by pushing them full up until locked flush with the forward beam. If necessary, the stow assist handle can be used to assist in stowing the ladder by releasing the handle and pushing the ladder to the stowed position and pushing the stow assist handle to the closed (stowed) position and releasing it.

The ladder is extended remotely by opening the ground power receptacle door and holding the ladder remote release switch (lower switch) to the down (deploy) position. The three latches are opened by a battery powered actuator. The

Aviation Boatswain's Mate (Handling) 3rd Class Bart Kooyman directs an F/A-18E Super Hornet assigned to the 'Kestrels' of Strike Fighter Squadron 137 (VFA-137) onto the number one bow catapult on the USS Abraham Lincoln (CVN 72). **US Navy/Mass Communication Specialist 2nd Class James Evans**

An F/A-18F Super Hornet assigned to the 'Red Rippers' of Strike Fighter Squadron 11 (VFA-11) launches from the number four waist catapult of the aircraft carrier USS Harry S. Truman (CVN 75) when underway in the Persian Gulf. The aircraft is loaded with a GBU-12 laser-guided bomb, and AGM-65 air-to-ground missile (both on the left-wing pylons) and a single JDAM munition on the right-wing pylon, a payload for close air support. **US Navy/Seaman Kevin Murray Jr**

Back in October 2015, VFA-41's CAG-bird was F/A-18F BuNo 166842/NH100. The aircraft is seen over Afghanistan loaded with a GBU-12 laser-guided bomb and a GBU-38 JDAM munition.
US Navy/Lt Kyle Terwilliger

An F/A-18F Super Hornet launches from the number three waist catapult of the aircraft carrier USS *Kitty Hawk* (CV 63) for the last time on August 6, 2008. Carrier Air Wing 5's aircraft flew off *Kitty Hawk* to join the USS *George Washington* (CVN 73). The *George Washington* replaced *Kitty Hawk* as the US Navy's only carrier operating from Japan. The *Kitty Hawk* headed back to the United States for decommissioning in early 2009.
US Navy/Mass Communication Specialist 3rd Class Kyle Gahlau

Sailors from Strike Fighter Squadron 103 (VFA-103) 'Jolly Rogers' direct an F/A-18F Super Hornet on the flight deck of the aircraft carrier USS *Dwight D. Eisenhower* (CVN 69) during a composite unit exercise (COMPTUEX), to evaluate capabilities and ensure readiness prior to deployment.
US Navy/Mass Communication Specialist 3rd Class Patrick Gearhiser

ladder drops to the open position while being restrained from free falling by a dampening strut (drop time approximately three to four seconds). All other procedures for securing the ladder are the same as manual opening.

Ejection Seat

The SJU-17(V)1/A, 2/A, and 9/A, and SJU-17A (V)1/A, 2/A, and 9/A NACES (Navy Aircrew Common Ejection Seat) are ballistic catapult/rocket systems that provide the pilot with a quick, safe, and positive means of escape from the aircraft.

The seat includes an initiation system which, after jettisoning the canopy and positioning the occupant for ejection, fires the telescopic seat catapult. Canopy breakers on the top of the seat give capability of ejecting through the canopy. As the seat departs the aircraft and the catapult reaches the end of the stroke, a rocket motor on the bottom of the seat is fired. The thrust of the rocket motor sustains the thrust of the catapult to eject the seat to a height sufficient for parachute deployment even if ejection is initiated at zero speed, zero altitude in a substantially level attitude.

F/A-18F Ejection Seat System

The ejection seats in the two-seat F/A-18F are ejected at opposite divergent angles to one another. The rear seat diverges to the left while the forward seat diverges to the right. The amount of divergence is influenced by the weight of the aircrew and the speed of the ejection. The heavier the aircrew and the faster the speed the less the resulting divergent angle. In addition, a sequencing system is installed to allow dual ejection initiated from either cockpit or single (aft) seat ejection initiated from the rear cockpit. A command selector valve is installed in the rear cockpit to control whether ejection from the rear cockpit is dual or single.

DEFENSIVE SYSTEMS
Electronic Warfare Survivability Package

The Super Hornet's electronic warfare (EW) suite is built around the ALQ-214 IDECM (integrated defensive countermeasures) system and its RFCM (radio frequency countermeasures) system.

IDECM provides the aircrew with co-ordinated situational awareness and manages on-board and off-board deception countermeasures, expendable decoys and signal and frequency control of emissions. It is used to counter enemy air defences in a defensive manner.

IDECM includes the Symetrics Industries ALE-47 countermeasures dispenser system capable of dispensing chaff cartridges, flares, POET (Primed Oscillator Expendable Transponder) and GEN-X (Generic Expendable) decoys. It carries 120 expendable decoys versus 60 carried in the ALE-39 fitted on legacy Hornets and allows the pilot to optimise the countermeasures employed against threats in any of the release modes - manual, semi-automatic and automatic.

In automatic mode the system receives threat data from the aircraft's survivability sensors (missile warning system, radar warning receiver) and then selects the appropriate response - type, sequence, pattern, and timing. In semi-automatic mode the system provides a signal to the pilot who must consent to dispensation. Manual mode has six pre-programmed responses that the pilot can choose from to defeat the threat.

The IDECM resource manager integrates all countermeasures combining expendables and jamming in co-ordinated techniques cutting wasteful dispensation of expendables.

The Raytheon ALE-50 is an integrated towed decoy for long-range detection and fast deployment against most radar-guided threats. It acts as a preferential target that lures enemy missiles away with a radar cross-section larger than the aircraft.

The ALR-67(V)3 radar warning receiver (RWR) provides warning of detected threat emitters that are targeting the aircraft. It intercepts, identifies, and prioritises threat signals characterised in terms of frequency, amplitude, direction, and pulse width. Unlike the earlier ALR-67(V)2, a super-heterodyne receiver fitted on the legacy Hornet, the (V)3 is a digital-queued receiver providing the Super Hornet with greater sensitivity throughout a wider frequency range. The ALR-67(V)3 has a programmed library of threat frequencies and waveforms. Upon detection of a threat, the (V)3 displays symbology about the threat. Based on the type of waveform detected the ALR-67(V)3 provides either a non-lethal, lethal, or critical categorisation with its direction of arrival.

The ALR-67(V)3 is a quadrant system with two forward antennas built into the leading-edge flaps on the lex (the forward component of the wing leading to the fuselage) and one in each of the vertical stabilisers. It also features a low-band array on the underside of the aircraft.

On the legacy Hornet, each component of the EW suite was run independently requiring a high level of operator interaction. The ALR-67(V)3 is an integrated system. A central computer in the onboard jammer (the resource manager of the IDECM suite) communicates with the ALR-67(V)3 to establish the active threats in the battle space. Using its own receiver, the ALR-67(V)3 compares and combines threats to optimise a co-ordinated response, such as jamming and chaff dispensation.

Onboard RF (Radio Frequency) jamming capability is provided by the ALQ-214

equipped with its own receiver and three receive-antennas. The ALQ-214 determines if the onboard system can respond to a threat. If the desired countermeasure technique is available, the system will invoke an omni-directional response that includes Directed Infra-Red Countermeasure (DIRCM). The system operates in manual, semi-automatic or automatic mode. In manual mode the operator commands the system to jam from the display showing the threat. In semi-automatic mode the system presents a queue of detected threats, the operator must give consent for it to jam. In automatic mode the system jams without any consent.

Aircrew get feedback, enhanced symbology appears on the cockpit display, so they can see the jamming in progress, coordinated with their manoeuvring.

The ALQ-214 passed OPEVAL in 2004 and was first fielded in the fleet with Strike Fighter Squadron 154 (VFA-154) 'Black Knights'.

Integrated with the onboard jammer is an off-board jamming system - the ALE-55 fibre-optic towed decoy (FOTD). It works coherently and synergistically with the onboard system to defeat threats throughout the RF spectrum in three layers of defence - suppression, deception, and seduction.

During a tracking-radar's acquisition phase, the Super Hornet's EW system uses the FOTD to emit jamming techniques through its broad-beam antennas. These suppress the radar's ability to acquire and track the aircraft.

If the tracking-radar successfully acquires the aircraft despite suppression, the ALE-55 uses deception techniques. Once the tracking-radar's signals are analysed, the ALE-55 determines the optimum jamming techniques to break the track. If multiple radars are detected, simultaneous jamming techniques can be transmitted. If a missile is launched the ALE-55 can break the missile's track of the aircraft or lure the missile away by becoming the target.

The ALE-55 subsystem comprises an on-board signal conditioning assembly and the FOTD. RF frequencies are converted to light by the signal conditioning assembly and transferred through the fibre-optic line. In primary mode the onboard EW system detects and analyses a threat, determines the appropriate response, and sends that response down the line to the FOTD for transmission. A back-up mode uses an independent repeater that modulates the detected signal and sends it down the line for transmission by the FOTD. A magazine mounted mid-body on the centreline of the underbelly houses three towed-decoys which can be deployed in manual, semi-automatic or automatic modes.

The FOTD has variable drag fins, which open and close in response to air pressure and speed. This ensures stable flight at all altitudes and airspeeds, reliable jamming performance and minimises tension on the fibre-optic line. The speed and precision of the decoy's deployment is achieved by an active braking system.

There are three blocks of IDECM each with a higher degree of integration. Block 1, the first to be fielded, featured the ALQ-165 onboard

F/A-18F Super Hornet BuNo 166613/AG203 from Strike Fighter Squadron 103 (VFA-103) 'Jolly Rogers' breaks away from the wingman jet on April 29, 2009, during a close air support mission over Afghanistan. The aircraft flew the mission from the USS Dwight D. Eisenhower (CVN 69) in support of Operation Enduring Freedom. **US Navy/Lt Charlie Escher**

jammer. Block 2, currently fielded in the fleet, features the onboard ALQ-214 jammer and a resource manager. Using it cooperatively with the ALE-50 towed decoy enables simultaneous onboard and off board jamming. The next Block 3 version features more integration improvements including the ALE-55 fibre-optic towed decoy, which was in operational test and evaluation in late 2006.

Jammers are accessible from a fuselage door located forward of the port side engine - all components are located there.

TACTICAL SYSTEMS
Joint Helmet Mounted Cueing System

The Joint Helmet Mounted Cueing System (JHMCS) comprises a regular helmet and a HDU (helmet display unit). Each HDU visor is ground around the specific mask of the pilot or WSO, so it fits and locks down in position. The HDU must correctly align with the face and line of sight to ensure the symbology is displayed in the correct portion of the visor. JHMCS senses where the crewmember is looking with magnetic mapping - the tracking of distortions made by the operator's eyes in the visor's magnetic field.

JHMCS was originally designed for getting tally on targets in the air-to-air role. The HDU projects an exact representation of the HUD (head up display) onto the visor in front of the right eye wherever the pilot or WSO looks. The visor display blanks out when the pilot 'comes in' - looks back inside the cockpit at the HUD.

In operation, JHMCS was found to have application for the air-to-ground mission.

Software was subsequently developed for controlling the FLIR with JHMCS. This capability allows a ground target to be designated using JHMCS making the system a desired tool for crew coordination in the F-model.

With JHMCS each of the two-man crew has a small star projected on the visor showing each other's line of sight. Wherever the pilot looks, the WSO sees the pilot's star in his helmet field of view and vice versa. A small cross hair projected on the visor marks the spot where the crewmember is looking. When the cross-hair lines up with the star both crewmembers are looking at the same spot.

During FAC(A) this reduces the amount of communication and avoids mistakes when determining who is looking at what, increasing the crew's situational awareness.

JHMCS is integrated with the radar and ATFLIR. If the pilot or WSO looks at an adversary, the radar slews to it for a lock on.

Similarly, the FLIR is also slaved to the helmet. The visor presents a field of view and a small box used to zoom in and out during target acquisition. A crewmember can slew the FLIR on to the target, 'come in' to the cockpit and view the actual FLIR video, tighten it up and data link the FLIR video target designation to a GFAC. A revolutionary tool for air-to-ground missions.

JHMCS achieved initial operating capability in 2004. All F-model Super Hornets built up to Lot 28 had JHMCS in the front seat only. In November 2005, VX-31 commenced JHMCS aft cockpit integration using F/A-18F aircraft retrofitted with the ACS. The modified aircraft were the first to feature dual-cockpit JHMCS capability.

All Super Hornets built in Lot 30 upward are equipped with dual-cockpit JHMCS and earlier build F-models were retrofitted with dual-cockpit JHMCS.

Cockpit Displays

The Super Hornet has an UFCD (up front control display) - the primary interface with the aircraft's avionics systems - with touch-pad controller for waypoint or frequency entry.

Two DDIs (digital display indicators) are mounted on either side of the UFCD. Each DDI has 20 buttons positioned around the four edges of the screen, each with several functions.

The primary navigation-aid display is the MPCD (multipurpose colour display) located beneath the UFCD. It combines the horizontal situation indicator and a moving map.

All the displays use Active-Matrix Liquid Crystal Display technology. Software provides the capability to fuse MIDS, RWR and digital moving map on the displays.

Block II aircraft are equipped with the Advanced Mission Computer and DECD (digital expandable colour display) to replace the multipurpose colour display.

Advanced Crew Station

Advanced Crew Station (ACS) is the redesigned rear-cockpit for F-model Super Hornets. The front and rear-cockpits are decoupled so that the pilot and WSO can work independently of each other. The F/A-18F has a UFCD - the primary interface with the aircraft's avionics systems and two DDIs also referred to as hand controllers mounted on either side of the UFCD. The DDIs mirror each other in terms of functionality and allows the operator to control two displays at once.

With the ACS each DDI controls different functions providing the operator with greater capability. ACS has an 8in x 10in MPCD in place of the original 6in x 6in display. The larger screen displays more information including

F/A-18 SUPER HORNET

Strike Fighter Squadron 102's CAG-bird F/A-18F BuNo 165894/NF100 launches from the aircraft carrier *USS George Washington* (CVN 73) on August 24, 2009. At the time, the *George Washington* was the only permanently forward deployed aircraft carrier, homeported at Yokosuka, Japan. **US Navy/Mass Communication Specialist Christopher Harte**

moving map, MIDS tracks within 'a big piece of airspace' and FLIR imagery for searching for small targets.

ACS has a better cockpit lay out and all the caution warning lights required by the WSO in the rear-cockpit for safe operation of the aircraft.

Cockpit Independence
With ACS, the WSO in the rear-cockpit can launch missiles and release air-to-ground weapons. During ingress to a target, the pilot can focus on looking out for threats and other aircraft while the WSO arms the laser and drops the weapon.

All Lot 30 F-models have ACS fully integrated with JHMCS in the front and rear-cockpits.

Using a fully integrated ACS-JHMCS FA-18F in air combat with the ability to work JHMCS from the rear-cockpit against multiple targets enables the pilot and WSO to engage different targets near simultaneously from their decoupled cockpits.

New HOTAS options are available for the FAC(A) mission. It was difficult, sometimes impossible, for the WSO to assign DiMPIS (desired mean point of impact) with the hand controllers in the original rear-cockpit. The ACS enables the WSO to assign DiMPIS with target points and run the mission. The WSO can locate small targets using FLIR imagery displayed on the larger display. Using JHMCS the WSO can designate the target for other aircraft on the MIDS link, so those crews can see the target.

APG-79 Radar
The APG-79 AESA (active electronically scanned array) radar is designed to support FORCEnet, the US Navy's fully networked battle space. Built with secure, interoperable technology, the APG-79 enhances sharing of information with manned, unmanned, and ground-based systems for close cooperation on the battlefield. It provides the capability to perform as an essential node in the air and ground information network.

Radar Function
Raytheon's APG-79 AESA radar has an agile active electronic beam that swishes through multiple antennas in tile-array architecture close to the speed of light to perform the scan traditionally undertaken by a moving antenna.

The APG-79 uses a transmit-receive (TR) module positioned in front of the array, with high-power and low-noise amplifiers, which generate power during transmission. The combined power of the many TR modules on the front of the array is down converted from RF to digital and collimated, the antenna beam is formed (phase-up of the array) and the energy transmitted. Formation of the beam is electronically controlled by a gimble-array.

High speed beam steering (much greater than a mechanically controlled gimble) is facilitated by solid-state electronics. High-speed beam re-steer benefits interleaving of air-to-air and air-to-ground modes, which maintains airspace situational awareness while air-to-ground operations are undertaken. The multimode interleaving and net-centric capabilities of the APG-79 offer substantially increased situational awareness.

An advanced four-channel receiver/exciter gives the APG-79 wide bandwidth capability and the ability to generate a broad spectrum of waveforms for air-to-air, air-to-ground, and electronic warfare missions.

The APG-79 radar can track significantly more targets than current radar systems and can operate in multiple air-to-air and air-to-ground modes simultaneously. The modes are real beam mapping, synthetic aperture radar (air-to-air and air-to-ground SAR imagery), air-to-air search, air-to-air track, sea surface search, ground moving target indication and ground moving target tracking. In response to mission requirements, the radar's built-in resource manager automatically schedules tasks to optimise radar functions and minimise aircrew workload.

One key attribute of the APG-79 radar is its reliability - it has no moving parts (mechanical gimbles), which eliminates risk of failure.

A sailor signals the shooter as an F/A-18F Super Hornet assigned to the 'Flying Eagles' of Strike Fighter Squadron 122 (VFA-122) launches from the aircraft carrier *USS John C. Stennis* (CVN 74), when underway off the coast of Southern California. **US Navy/Mass Communication Specialist 2nd Class Walter Wayman**

F/A-18F Super Hornet BuNo 165875/SD120 assigned to Air Test and Evaluation Squadron 23 (VX-23) 'Salty Dogs'. In 2010, the aircraft was dubbed the Green Hornet for a flight test programme focussed on increased use of alternative fuels, a blend of biofuel and conventional fuel. **US Navy/Liz Goettee**

The ultra-thin, light antennas have a low failure rate, with no maintenance predicted for 10 to 20 years. Raytheon claims that the APG-79 yields a five-fold increase by comparison to the APG-73 radar fitted in legacy Hornets.

The APG-79 provides the Super Hornet with an electronic attack capability with air-to-air and air-to-ground elements. Defensive electronic countermeasure techniques used for electronic attack, generated by the ALQ-214 jammer are sent to the APG-79 via an RF connection and directed to the target through the radar's TR modules.

Running the APG-79 with H4 software enabled more air-to-air capabilities and network centric operations. An improved automatic target identification system called ATRATC (Auto Target Recognition and Auto Target Cueing), and more sensor integration followed.

APG-79 Evolution

Boeing selected Raytheon to develop a AESA radar for the Super Hornet in mid-November 1999. VX-31 flew the first Super Hornet fitted with an APG-79 radar at Naval Air Weapons Station China Lake in June 2003. In early September 2003, Boeing received a US$49.5m contract for eight low-rate initial production (LRIP) APG-79 radar systems

Between 2004-2005, four LRIP APG-79 AESA radars fitted in Lot 26 Super Hornets were assigned to VX-31 and VX-9 at China Lake as part of an integrated test and evaluation programme. The first sorties using interleaved air-to-air and air-to-ground modes were flown there in March 2004 as part of the integration effort.

In mid-2005 the APG-79 test programme shifted focus from pure radar integration to weapon system integration.

On August 3, 2005, an APG-79-equipped Super Hornet dropped the first JDAM over the China Lake range. The weapon was delivered using high-resolution SAR (synthetic aperture radar) imagery, generated by the APG-79 radar, to designate the target. The coordinates were passed to the JDAM, which successfully impacted the target, corrected with navigation data provided by the INS system, during its flight to the target.

The initial AIM-120 AMRAAM live-fire occurred on October 19, 2005, against a Naval Air Systems Command drone. This was an end test to ensure successful integration of aircraft, APG-79 radar, AIM-120 missile and the aircraft's mission computer. Successfully acquiring the target and committing a kill required a solid performance by the APG-79 in air-to-air mode. In the event the APG-79 provided the AIM-120 missile with solid-detection and tracking of the target, which in turn performed well in tracking the drone target to impact.

Six days later, the APG-79 scored kills against two targets on a dual JDAM drop. Both targets were struck within the distances required to classify them as destroyed. The October 25 mission successfully demonstrated the APG-79's ability to generate target coordinates from SAR imagery for two targets, each hit by a different JDAM weapon.

Further strike and network capability was proven on February 17, 2006, when two non-AESA equipped Super Hornets dropped four 2,000lb JDAM weapons on four different targets.

An APG-79 equipped F/A-18F tasked as an armed reconnaissance platform, generated a long-range, high-resolution synthetic aperture radar map. That map was used to designate four closely spaced stationary targets and successfully demonstrated 'through the weather targeting' capability.

Target coordinates were then data linked to the two-strike aircraft via MIDS. All four targets, located within proximity to each other, were hit and classed as destroyed. The AESA-equipped Super Hornet then acquired highly detailed bomb damage assessments. This was the first-time target coordinates generated by one Super Hornet were passed via data link to other aircraft.

The successful completion of the mission using MIDS and JDAM weapons was critical to verify the AESA radar as a force multiplier.

On April 12, 2006, the development test team at China Lake conducted an AIM-120 AMRAAM live-fire against multiple manoeuvring targets. The Super Hornet successfully demonstrated the APG-79's ability to engage, lock-on and launch two AMRAAMs data linked from the aircraft against two highly manoeuvrable targets.

The AESA radar maintained track on the targets and reported the tracking information via data link through to successful impact.

In mid-May 2006, the final AMRAAM live-fire missions were flown against multiple targets (drones) - a major milestone in preparation for the APG-79 OPEVAL, which commenced in July 2006.

The first Super Hornet equipped with the APG-79, a Lot 27 aircraft, was rolled out at Boeing's production plant in St Louis on April 21, 2005, one of eight delivered in FY2005. In FY2008 all 42 Super Hornets delivered under Lot 30 were fitted with the APG-79. A AESA-equipped Super Hornet has an enhanced

In 2010, Strike Fighter Squadron 137 (VFA-137) 'Kestrels' operated a CAG-bird with a pixelated camouflage scheme. The aircraft is seen launching form the USS *Abraham Lincoln* (CVN 72) for an in-flight change of command ceremony. **US Navy/Mass Communication Specialist 3rd Class Lex Wenberg**

F/A-18 SUPER HORNET

Smoke swirls off the nose wheel tyres of an F/A-18F Super Hornet during an arrested landing on board the aircraft carrier USS Ronald Reagan (CVN 76) when underway in the Arabian Sea. US Navy/Mass Communication Specialist 3rd Class Alexander Tidd

An F/A-18E Super Hornet being directed onto the number one bow catapult on the aircraft carrier USS George Washington (CVN 73) during Exercise Talisman Sabre 2011, a bilateral training event between Australian and US forces. US Navy/Mass Communication Specialist 2nd Class Adam Thomas

forward fuselage built with composite skins to provide greater cooling to the APG-79 radar and avionics.

First AESA-Equipped Squadron: VFA-213 'Black Lions'

Fighter Squadron 213 (VF-213) 'Black Lions' returned from deployment aboard the USS *Theodore Roosevelt* with the F-14D on March 10, 2006. On April 15, the squadron commenced transition to the Block II F/A-18F Super Hornet at Naval Air Station Oceana, Virginia as Strike Fighter Squadron 213 (VFA-213). Squadron pilots completed carrier qualifications on the *Theodore Roosevelt* on October 18 and achieved safe for flight on October 27, 2006.

VFA-213 was the first Super Hornet squadron to operate aircraft equipped with the APG-79 AESA radar. It was selected purely because of its timing in the fleet transition to Super Hornet.

VFA-106 'Gladiators', the Atlantic Fleet Super Hornet FRS managed VFA-213's transition to the AESA-equipped Super Hornet. VFA-106 took delivery of six AESA-equipped aircraft so that VFA-213 aircrew were able to undertake most of their event training in AESA-equipped F/A-18Fs. Most events in the fighter weapons phase of the transition course were flown using refined tactics because of the APG-79's greater capabilities.

Commander Dan Kay, the man leading VFA-213 at the time explained: "As the first AESA squadron we are like a test-bed unit for determining the radar's employment." US Navy personnel from Top Gun, the Fighter Weapons School based at Naval Air Station Fallon, Nevada, and the VX community made recommendations. Much of the work undertaken by VFA-213 working with VFA-106 was focused on writing the NATOPS documentation for tactics and employment of the APG-79 radar.

VFA-213 deployed to Naval Air Station Fallon, Nevada in the first quarter of 2007 to work with Top Gun and finalise the recommendations for APG-79 NATOPS. The squadron entered the flying phase of the inter deployment training cycle in the fourth quarter of 2007

In early January 2007, VFA-213 received its 11th Lot 28, Block II F/A-18F aircraft - the most advanced in the fleet.

PODS
ASQ-228 ATFLIR

In November 1997, Boeing selected the Hughes Aircraft Company based at El Segundo, California, (later acquired by Raytheon) to develop an Advanced Targeting Forward-Looking Infra-Red (ATFLIR) sensor for the Super Hornet. Ten pods were built under an EMD contract for qualification and flight-testing. Low-rate initial production of 14 ATFLIR pods and spares followed the award of a US$69m US Navy contract in March 2001.

Raytheon's ASQ-228 ATFLIR (Advanced Targeting Forward-Looking Infra-Red) is a third-generation precision targeting pod.

ATFLIR consists of a 3-to-5-micron focal plane targeting FLIR, an electro-optic camera, a high-powered laser spot tracker, a navigation FLIR and a CCD (charged couple device) TV camera. Different fields of zoom of the TV camera are incorporated with the IR image.

There are three modes of operation - point-stabilise mode, seen-track mode, or auto-track mode - all incorporated with a laser for target tracking, ranging and target-designation.

In July 2005, VX-31 successfully engaged a remote-controlled truck with a 2,000lb JDAM fitted with a UHF data link. The crew of the F/A-18F used an ATFLIR to continuously track the target, generate real-time target updates and link them to the JDAM during its flight using the Digital Communication System. The aircraft's weapon management system guided the inert JDAM within two metres of the target.

The latest ATFLIR pods have a real-time ROVER-capable data link for the FAC(A) role. An image captured by the FLIR can be annotated and data linked to ground troops who can view it in real-time. Instructions can be sent to the cockpit advising the crew on where the troops require the weapon to go. This eases target acquisition and avoids confusion.

In March 2006, operational Super Hornets received a real-time streaming video capability for ATFLIR, a requirement that arose from operations in Iraq. Boeing developed the capability in 81 days from receipt of task at the end of November 2005 to deployment in Iraq. Known as ATFLIR streaming video, the solution involved adding a single board of transmitters and amplifiers onto the aircraft, using existing antennas to transmit video. Streaming-live video capability allows ground troops to watch the same FLIR video as seen by the aircrew.

The ATFLIR road map includes improvements to stabilise the TV picture and incorporation of an IR-marker.

ATFLIR achieved initial operating capability with VFA-14 and VFA-41 in April 2003.

ANAV (accurate navigation) is an EGI (embedded GPS/inertial) navigation system designed for integration and operation with the ATFLIR pod, and the APG-79 radar. It provides the crew with precise geo-location.

ASD-12 SHARP

Raytheon's ASD-12 SHARP (Shared High Altitude Reconnaissance Pod) is a multipurpose reconnaissance pod carried on the centreline station. It is comparable in size and shape to a fuel tank without the pure elliptical form. SHARP operates in either manual or a pre-planned mode with simultaneous airborne and ground reconnaissance capability.

The mid-body is a rotating component housing the camera and lens. In pre-planned mode, target positions are programmed into SHARP using a planning station prior to the mission. Aircrew designate a route to fly and assign targets that require imagery. The planning station calculates if the pod's required field of view is available.

Once the aircraft is airborne, target information is shown on the display. The crew can see the designated route, what is being captured, what will be captured next and what was missed.

SHARP recognises the sequential target order along the designated route. As the aircraft approaches the target area the mid-body rotates toward the target at the depression angle to capture the required images. It calculates when to start and stop capturing images accordingly. Target geo-location is fed to the SHARP pod from the aircraft's EGI navigation system.

SHARP also provides feedback. On return to the carrier the pod provides exact coverage details for all the targets. If a target was not sufficiently covered the system advises a re-run. A stepping capability allows SHARP to cover a target area by acquiring a patchwork of images. By designating a target with the required coverage, the system calculates how many images are required to cover the area.

In manual mode the pilot simply points the pod left or right along the route. This is often

Aviation Boatswain's Mate (Fuel) Airman Samuel Huff refuels an F/A-18E Super Hornet using the single point refuelling receptacle on the flight deck of the USS *John C. Stennis* (CVN 74). **US Navy/Mass Communication Specialist 3rd Class Kenneth Abbate**

used with flexible tasking when a particular area requires investigation.

SHARP Operations

The first fully operational deployment of SHARP was made by VFA-22 and VFA-115 embarked on the USS *Ronald Reagan* between January and July 2006. The all-digital pod was used for NTISR (non-traditional intelligence, surveillance, and reconnaissance) missions. Squadron personnel were uploading and downloading the pods on and off the jets, while Raytheon representatives performed system maintenance. Imagery captured by the SHARP pods was analysed by Navy personnel assigned to the *Reagan*'s intelligence centre. The system also enabled pilots to data link imagery in near real-time, either to troops on the ground in Iraq or to the Combined Air Operations Center at Al Udeid Air Base in Qatar.

Aerial Refuelling Store

The Super Hornet's air-refuelling store (ARS) is a pod housing a hose and drogue mechanism, carried on the centreline station for the tanker mission. The ARS has undergone upgrade with an improved power system known as ARSIPS featuring an improved Ram Air Turbine and other sub-systems. VX-23 undertook 'cats and traps' testing of the ARSIPS pod on the F/A-18E and F/A-18F to evaluate the pod for launch and recovery from a carrier flight deck.

The air-refuelling capability within a carrier air wing, known as organic mission tanking, once undertaken by the S-3B Viking is now conducted by Super Hornet squadrons. That mission involves tanking other strike aircraft en route to and recovery from the battlefield.

Tanker missions are generally flown with a three-wet configuration - the ARS and two 480-gallon drop tanks. Full tanker capability is flown with a five-wet configuration (four 480-gallon drop tanks and the ARS). Allowing for a 4,000lb reserve fuel load, required by the pilot 'on the ball' to land, an F/A-18E can provide 19,000lb of offload fuel but only when the tanker remains close to the carrier. Total offload drops by an average 5,000lb for every hour the tanker remains airborne. Offload is also affected by the duration of the carrier's launch-recovery cycle and the air-refuelling position relative to the ship.

NAVAIR continues to expand the Super Hornet's tanking envelope at higher and lower speeds. The ability to tank at slow speeds means the Super Hornet can support all aircraft within a carrier air wing including the E-2 Hawkeye.

FACTS ABOUT THE SUPER HORNET

Super Hornet Fact
To differentiate between an F/A-18 Hornet and F/A-18 Super Hornet during flight deck operations, cats and traps, sailors gave the Rhino nickname to the Super Hornet.

Rhino Fact
All F/A-18E and F/A-18F Super Hornets built from Lot 26 and upward are fitted with the APG-79 AESA radar, 135 as retrofits, 280 forward fitted. All 415 aircraft were configured to full Block II configuration.

Rhino Fact
Boeing test pilot Phil Pirozzi clocked the 1,000th flight-hour flown by Super Hornets in F/A-18F2 on May 5, 1997, during a test flight to fire an AIM-120 AMRAAM.

Rhino Fact
Lt Tom Hole launched an AIM-9 Sidewinder missile from F/A-18F2 on April 5, 1997, the first missile fired from a Super Hornet.

Rhino Fact
During the first 3,000 flight hours, the Integrated Test Team evaluated 26 different weapon load configurations, fired 25 missiles, dropped over 430,000lb of ordnance and completed over 1,400 aerial refuelling operations.

Rhino Fact
The first production Super Hornet, F/A-18E6 BuNo 165533, completed its maiden flight from St Louis Lambert Field, Missouri on November 6, 1998.

Rhino Fact
On March 14, 1999, F/A-18F1 and F2 completed sea trials aboard USS Harry S Truman (CVN 75). During the trials, on March 8, 1999, an F/A-18F undertook the first night launch and recovery.

Rhino Fact
Development testing of the APG-79 AESA radar was completed by VX-31 in June 2006. OPEVAL commenced with VX-9 in July and finished in November 2006.

Rhino Fact
The US Navy declared initial operational capability on the ASQ-228 ATFLIR with VFA-102 'Rattlesnakes' at Naval Air Station Lemoore, California in mid-September 2003.

Rhino Fact
Boeing received a US$8.9bn multiyear contract for 222 Super Hornets on June 16, 2000. The five-year contract comprised 36 aircraft in FY2000, 42 in FY2001 and 48 in FY2002-2004.

Rhino Fact
Strike Fighter Squadron 115 (VFA-115) 'Eagles' commenced transition to the F/A-18E in December 2000 - the first fleet squadron to operate Super Hornet.

Rhino Fact
The first combat strikes flown by the Super Hornet were made by VFA-115 'Eagles' over southern Iraq on November 6, 2002.

Rhino Fact
Strike Fighter Squadron 115 (VFA-115) landed 12 F/A-18E Super Hornets aboard the USS Abraham Lincoln (CVN-72) on July 24, 2002, starting the Super Hornets maiden deployment.

Rhino Fact
At the end of 2004, VFA-122's weekly sortie generation was up to 350 sorties per week.

Rhino Fact
VFA-27 commenced transition on June 1, 2004. Achieved safe for flight in mid-September. Resumed operations at Naval Air Facility Atsugi with 13 F/A-18Es by October 1, 2004.

Rhino Fact
VFA-122, the Super Hornet training squadron received its first seven Super Hornets at an arrival ceremony at Naval Air Station Lemoore on November 17, 1999.

Rhino Fact
Safe for flight qualification is a shore-based inspection during which evaluators make sure a squadron can fly and maintain the aircraft with all programmes in place.

Rhino Fact
The US Navy awarded Boeing a second multiyear production contract for 210 Super Hornets valued at US$48.6bn and a US$1bn system design and development for the EA-18G airborne electronic attack aircraft on December 29, 2003. The US Navy purchased 42 aircraft between FY2005 and 2009.

Rhino Fact
Super Hornets are delivered to the US Navy in Lot numbers tied to the respective Fiscal Year. Lot 28 aircraft were delivered in FY2006. Delivery of Lot 29 aircraft commenced in July 2006, three months ahead of schedule including 22 AESA-equipped aircraft.

Rhino Fact
The first Block II Super Hornet, a Lot 27 aircraft, featuring the APG-79 AESA radar, the latest mission computer suite and 8in x 10in display in the aft cockpit was rolled out from Boeing's St Louis facility on April 25, 2005.

Rhino Fact
By April 30, 2006, Boeing had delivered 273 Super Hornet (257 as of December 31, 2005) aircraft to the US Navy.

ORDNANCE

MISSILES

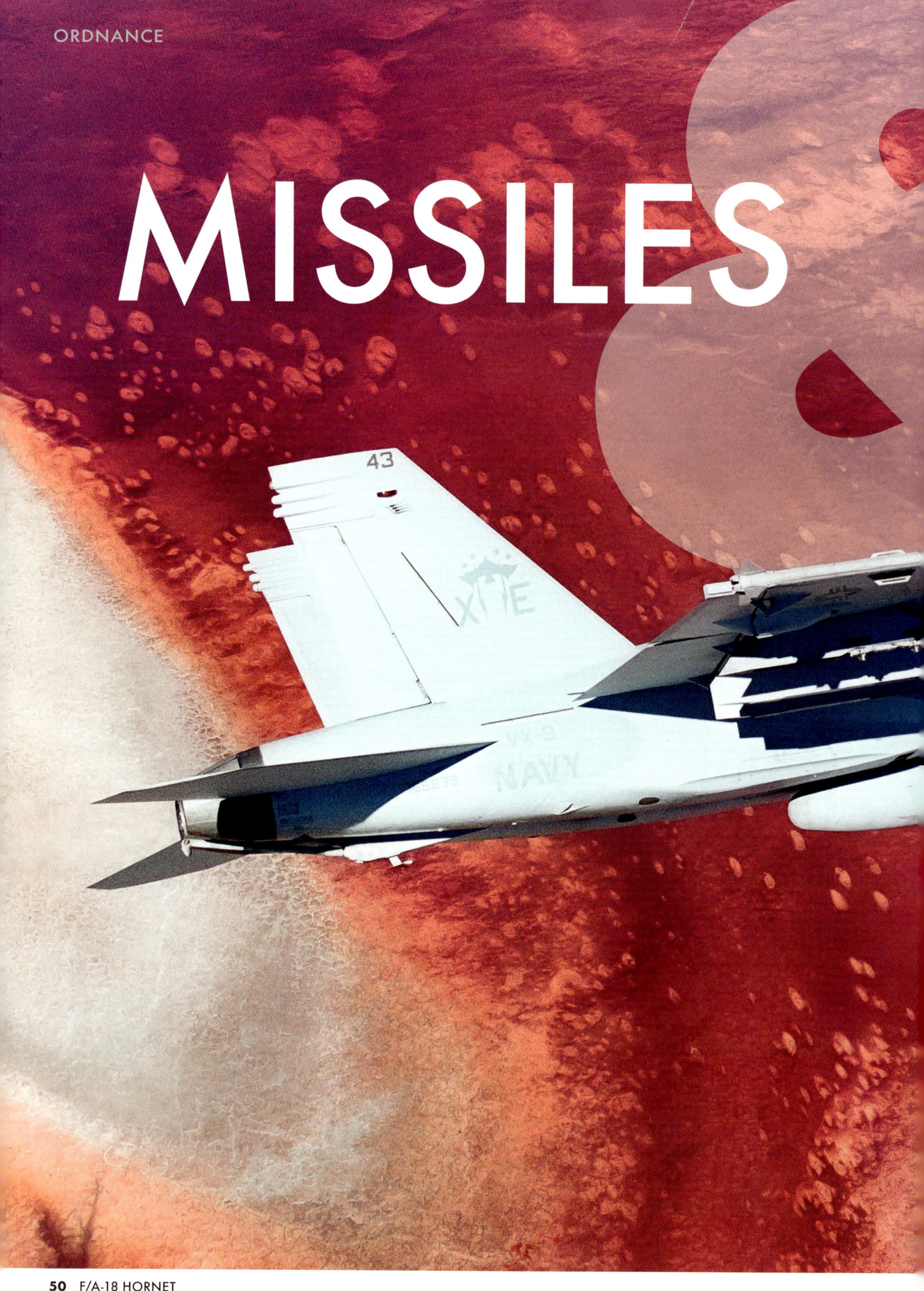

50 F/A-18 HORNET

Mark Ayton details the F/A-18 Super Hornet's missile and munitions arsenal, its operational test programme, the Block II, and the latest test programmes of the Block III variant.

MUNITIONS

F/A-18F Super Hornet BuNo 166639/XE243 assigned to Air Test and Evaluation Squadron 9 (VX-9) 'Vampires' conducts an operation test mission, while over Owens Lake in the vast eastern High Sierra and Mojave test ranges. This aircraft was one of the first Super Hornets equipped with the APG-79 active electronically scanned array radar.
US Navy/Cdr Ian Anderson

THE SUPER HORNET strike fighter employs a variety of missiles and munitions that include air intercept missiles (AIMs), air-to-ground missiles (AGMs), air-to-ground glided weapons, guided bomb units (GBUs) and GPS-guided direct attack munitions (JDAMs). We start the review with air intercept missiles.

AIM-7 Sparrow

The AIM-7 is a medium-range, all-weather, all-altitude radar-guided air-to-air missile armed with a high-explosive warhead. The missile has four sections: guidance, warhead, control, and rocket motor. Sparrow's configuration features a cylindrical fuselage, four wings at mid-body and four tail fins.
Dimensions: Length 147in, diameter 8in
Launcher: LAU-106

AIM-9X Sidewinder

The AIM-9X is a supersonic air-to-air guided missile with full day-night capability. It employs a passive infrared target acquisition system, proportional navigational guidance, a closed-loop position servo fin actuator unit (FAU), and a target detector.

Powered by a solid-propellant rocket motor, the AIM-9X is configured with an annular blast fragmentation warhead controlled by an electronic safe-arm device.

Four forward mounted fixed wings provide aerodynamic lift and stability. Airframe manoeuvring is achieved by four control fins, mounted in line with the fixed wings, and activated by the FAU.

Jet vane control provides enhanced manoeuvrability by deflecting rocket motor thrust to aid in turning.
Dimensions: Length 119in, diameter 5in
Launcher: LAU-127

AIM-120 AMRAAM

The AIM-120 is a medium range, radar-guided air-to-air missile with capability in both the beyond-visual-range and within-visual-range arenas by day and night. An AIM-120 has four component sections.

The guidance section houses the software and hardware required for target acquisition and tracking, navigation, data link processing, and electrical power distribution.

The armament section houses the warhead assembly and a booster threaded onto a safety and arming fuse device.

The propulsion section uses a single, reduced-smoke solid propellant in a boost-sustain configuration encased in an insulated steel case which is part of the airframe.

The control section consists of control electronics, actuator batteries, and four independently controlled servo-actuators.

The missile has four mid-body fixed wings, four moveable rear fins, and an umbilical connection which communicates with the launch aircraft for targeting and initialisation.

The latest AIM-120D model features improved kinematics, improved high off bore-sight capability, a GPS-enhanced inertial measurement unit and enhanced two-way data link. Compared to the AIM-120C-7, the AIM-120D reportedly has 50% greater range,

ORDNANCE

and better guidance throughout the missile's entire flight envelope to increase kill probability, with an expanded no-escape envelope.

The AIM-120D is subject to a series of four System Improvement Programs (SIP). SIP-1 was fielded in April 2017.

The US Air Force and US Navy completed operational test activities for the AIM-120D SIP-2 in January 2020 and fielded SIP-2 in February 2020.

The two services expected to begin operational test activities for the AIM-120D SIP-3 programme in February 2021 and complete operational testing in July 2021.
Dimensions: Length 144in, diameter 7in
Launcher: LAU-127

AGM-65 Maverick

Modular in design, the AGM-65 Maverick air-to-ground missile can be built with different combinations of the guidance section and warhead: three different seekers and two different warheads are available. All configurations use a common solid-rocket motor propulsion section.

Seeker options are electro-optical imaging, imaging infrared or laser guidance.

Warhead options are a 125lb shaped charge fired by a contact fuse or a 300lb penetrator with a delayed fuse to fire the warhead once the target has been penetrated. The warhead is housed in the missile's centre section.

The AGM-65 has a cylindrical body, long-chord delta wings and tail control surfaces mounted close to the trailing edge of the launch aircraft's wing.

Of the many variants of the AGM-65 missile, the US Navy tends to use the laser guidance AGM-65E and imaging infrared guidance AGM-65F, both with the penetrator warhead.
Dimensions: Length 97.7in, diameter 12in
Launcher: Either the LAU-88A for a three stick or the LAU-117A for a single weapon

AGM-84D Harpoon

The AGM-84 Harpoon is an all-weather, over the horizon, anti-ship missile effective against moving or stationary vessels ranging from patrol boats to ships.

The Harpoon has active radar guidance and the capability to cruise just above the surface toward its target and just before impact execute a terminal pop-up manoeuvre to counter close-in defences and enhance warhead penetration.

The missile has a 500lb warhead and a turbojet sustainer engine.
Dimensions: Length 172in, diameter 13.5in.
Rack: BRU-32 (Bomb Rack Unit)

AGM-84K SLAM-ER

The AGM-84K is a long-range weapon designed for day-night and adverse weather precision strike capability against high value land and sea targets. The AGM-84K has the name Standoff Land Attack Missile-Expanded Response or SLAM-ER. Network-enabled, the AGM-84k is used to strike pre-planned and opportunity moving, and stationary land and ship targets. It is equipped with a 500lb warhead, an infrared sensor, a data link, and a modified GPS receiver.

The SLAM-ER employs different operating modes to make it effective against fixed targets launched as either an autonomous fire-and-forget missile or a man-in-the loop weapon using the advanced data link.

Aircrew view real-time seeker IR video all the way to target impact, with the ability to redirect or abort if required.
Dimensions: Length 172in, diameter 13.5in
Rack: BRU-32

AGM-84L Harpoon Block II

The Block II Harpoon has an expanded target engagement envelope, greater resistance to electronic attack, and an improved targeting capability.

Armed with a 500lb penetration, high-explosive blast warhead, the Block II Harpoon is equipped with GPS-aided INS and the same low-cost inertial measurement as fitted to the Joint Direct Attack Munition series of munitions.

The missile's guidance control unit is fitted with a selective availability, anti-spoofing module GPS receiver which can be fitted with a data link for network-centric operations.

Block II is also equipped with the same software, mission computer, integrated GPS/INS, and GPS antenna and receiver as the AGM-84H SLAM-ER.

The AGM-84L is propelled by a turbojet solid propellant booster.
Dimensions: Length 172in, diameter 13.5in
Rack: BRU-32.

AGM-84N Harpoon Block II+

The latest variant of the Harpoon missile can receive in-flight updates from a Super Hornet via the network-enabled datalink which improves the targeting and engagement of moving maritime targets. Further improvements to the AGM-84L are a new guidance navigation

Plumes extend from the rocket motor of an AGM-88E Advanced Anti-Radiation Guided Missile after launch from VX-31's F/A-18D Hornet BuNo 164279/DD113 over the China Lake range. **Naval Air Systems Command**

unit with embedded GPS, improved target selectivity, an abort option, and reliability and survivability enhancements to the weapon system.
Dimensions: Length 172in, diameter 13.5in
Rack: BRU-32

AGM-88E AARGM

The AGM-88E AARGM is the follow-on to the AGM-88B/C High-Speed Anti-Radiation Missile (HARM). AARGM consists of a newly developed guidance section and a modified AGM-88B HARM control section. AARGM uses existing AGM-88B and AGM-88C HARM rocket motor section, warhead section, wings, and fins. The new guidance section is equipped with a more sensitive wideband passive digital anti-radiation homing (ARH) receiver, a conformal antenna array, an active millimetre wave radar (MMW), and an integrated broadcast service receiver. ARH improvements over the AGM-88 HARM series include an increased field of view and larger frequency range. GPS allows position accuracy in location, time, and weapon impact assessment transmissions, and the MMW radar technology allows target discrimination and guidance during the terminal flight phase.

The ARH in combination with the conformal antenna can geolocate emitting targets very quickly. The control section incorporates a GPS-aided INS weapon impact assessment transmitter which provides point-to-point capability.
Dimensions: Length 164in, diameter 10in
Launcher: LAU-118A

Left clockwise: Sailors assigned to Strike Fighter Squadron 213 (VFA-213) 'Black Lions' remove an AGM-88 missile from the outer pylon of an F/A-18F Super Hornet aboard the aircraft carrier *USS George H.W. Bush* (CVN 77). **US Navy/Naval Air Crewman 3rd Class Joshua Horton**

An aviation ordnanceman performs maintenance on an 20mm M61A2 cannon. **US Navy/Mass Communication Specialist Robert Winn**

Aviation ordnancemen remove the M61 Vulcan cannon from an F/A-18E Super Hornet for a routine inspection.
US Navy/Mass Communication Specialist Joe Painter

Sailors secure an AIM-9X Sidewinder aerial intercept missile to an F/A-18E Super Hornet assigned to Strike Fighter Squadron 11 (VFA-11) 'Red Rippers' aboard the aircraft carrier *USS Enterprise* (CVN 65).
US Navy/Mass Communication Specialist Jesse Gonzalez

AARGM is employed by the F/A-18E, F/A-18F and EA-18G platforms.

AARGM Block 0 was intended for initial operational capability while the Block 1 upgrade was intended to deliver full operational capability, including Block 0 capability improvements, and an integrated broadcast service receiver (which enables reception of national broadcast data), and software changes to provide deferred capability requirements and address deficiencies identified during IOT&E.

In Q2 FY2010, the US Navy issued a change to the AARGM Capability Production Document (CPD) due to limitations discovered during developmental testing, which delayed the start of IOT&E until Q3 FY2010 to allow correction of system deficiencies; deferred a KPP (key performance parameter) target requirement to FOT&E; and clarified the acceptable target environment and reactive targeting constraints for IOT&E.

Commander, Operational Test and Evaluation Force (COTF) commenced AARGM IOT&E in June 2010, but less than three months later, the US Navy de-certified AARGM from IOT&E after the programme suffered six operational mission failures during initial captive-carriage flight tests.

The AARGM programme spent most of FY2011 correcting hardware and software deficiencies discovered in developmental testing and during its first IOT&E attempt. In July 2011, the DOT&E approved an updated AARGM operational test plan and the US Navy re-initiated dedicated IOT&E in August 2011.

NAVAIR postponed two live-missile test events scheduled for October 2011 due to an emergent anomaly that caused a communication failure between the AARGM guidance and control sections. They identified a short-term solution for the problem and conducted the live-missile events during Q2 FY2012.

Immediately preceding a February 2012 test event involving two other live-missile shots, NAVAIR notified the DOT&E that the planned threat scenario would likely result in mission failure due to a classified AARGM deficiency. Without DOT&E consent, the US Navy modified the approved test scenario to alleviate the classified deficiency and proceeded with live-missile testing. DOT&E disagreed with the adjusted threat representation and subsequently assessed these events as operational failures.

AARGM Block 0 testing was adequate to support an evaluation of the weapon system's operational effectiveness and operational suitability. Block 0 was deemed operationally suitable but not operationally effective - as assessed the weapon had multiple deficiencies.

The Block 1 software-only upgrade was expected to address AARGM's performance shortfalls and provide full operational capability.

The contractor conducted flight tests in FY2014 and delivered sequential software versions R1.0, R2.0, and R2.1 to NAVAIR. Based on the delivery of software version R2.1 and the missile's performance during contractor testing, modelling and simulation analysis, NAVAIR's AARGM program manager authorised AARGM to enter IOT&E. This commenced in August 2014 and involved four captive-carriage test events. Based on analysis of the missile's performance data, NAVAIR determined that a software update was required and delayed the planned captive-carriage and live fire test events scheduled for the remainder of Q1 FY2015.

Using R2.1 software, Air Test and Evaluation Squadron 9 and 31 (VX-9 and VX-31) conducted Phase 1 of IOT&E between Q4 FY2014 and Q1 FY2015. Deficiencies were discovered, testing was halted, significant software updates were required, and an additional Phase 1a integrated test phase was introduced

Software version R2.2 was delivered in Q3 FY2015 and Phase 1a was conducted in Q3 and Q4 FY2015.

Phase 1 IOT&E continued during FY2015. Squadrons VX-9 and VX-31 conducted four test events comprising 79 captive-carriage test runs. NAVAIR deemed a software update necessary and subsequently stopped the remaining captive-carriage and live fire test events.

After the software corrections of earlier deficiencies were completed, VX-9 and VX-31 also conducted Phase 1a in FY2015, which involved 11 test events, comprising 228 captive-carriage test runs, and two live fire test shots. Both live fire test events successfully engaged their target, and the test objectives were achieved; the first involved a moving surface target on the Point Mugu Sea Range while the second was against a traditional air defence unit on the China Lake range.

Naval Air Systems Command completed the first live fire of an AGM-88G Advanced Anti-Radiation Guided Missile-Extended Range over the Point Mugu Sea Test Range off the coast of southern California on July 19, 2021. F/A-18F Super Hornet BuNo 166450/DD217 assigned to Air Test and Evaluation Squadron 31 (VX-31) 'Dust Devils' was the launch aircraft.
Naval Air Systems Command

F/A-18F BuNo 166636/XE245 assigned to Air Test and Evaluation Squadron 9 (VX-9) 'Vampires' loaded with an asymmetric load comprising an inert BDU-50 practice bomb on the right-side mid-board pylon and one live Mk82 general purpose bomb on each left side mid-board pylon.
US Navy/Cdr Ian Anderson

Navigational errors were noted on several occasions during Phase 1a, cause was identified, software changes were made and tested during Phase 2 IOT&E in Q1 FY2015.

The Block 1 Upgrade IOT&E conducted by VX-9 and VX-31 started in Q4 FY2014 and ended after DOT&E had rescinded approval of the Block 1 FOT&E test plan on June 13, 2016, because the US Navy had taken no significant actions to address the issues discovered with the guidance/navigation computer anomalies, poor reliability, and multiple software stability problems during integrated testing.

During a programme review on August 2, 2016, operational testers from VX-9, COTF and the DOT&E detailed numerous problems and deficiencies that were affecting weapon accuracy and declining reliability. All issues were well below the CPD requirements and raised concerns for the stability of the software despite multiple software changes (versions R2.1, R2.2, R2.2.1, R2.2.2, and R2.2.3) during the Block 1 Upgrade IOT&E.

The AARGM Program Office stated that it was meeting all KPPs, an achievement that was acknowledged by the operational testers who also pointed out that the missile was failing to meet a key reliability parameter and other significant CPD requirements, which were affecting system performance and accuracy, and significantly limiting the missile's effectiveness against many advanced threats and counter tactics against threat anti-radiation missiles (ARM). Operational testers also highlighted the instability of the software despite numerous changes made to the code.

The Program Office gained agreement from US Navy leadership which directed that testing continue. VX-9 and VX-31 completed test items from within the integrated evaluation framework as a developmental test assist to characterise the system from Q3 FY2016 to Q2 FY2017 at Naval Air Weapons Station China Lake, and Naval Base Ventura County, Point Mugu, California.

Eight live fire test events took place during Block 1 Upgrade testing.

Two were deemed failures. Each of the two missiles launched impacted the ground significant distances away from their intended target and had little to no weapons effect on the actual target. The failures were caused by several significant classified problems affecting the accuracy of the weapon. Because of the two failures, the DOT&E directed NAVAIR to develop an updated live fire test plan that would result in an acceptable level of statistical confidence.

NAVAIR completed testing of the AGM-88E AARGM Block 1 in March 2017, when VX-31 completed the final three of eight live fire test events. Six were deemed successful engagements and two failed (see above).

In total, the AARGM Block 1 FOT&E and developmental test assist periods consisted of 32 sorties and 234 flight hours consisting of 222 captive carry runs and eight live fire events. R2.2.3 was the final version of Block 1 software used during the FOT&E with just 24 hours of evaluation (from the 234 hours), and the version issued to the fleet.

The test team and OPTEVFOR observed 12 system of systems operational mission failures during the 234 flight hours, resulting in a system of systems reliability of 19.50 hours mean time between operational mission failures, well below the CPD-defined requirement of 28 hours or greater.

Four of the nine weapons delivered to China Lake had hardware failures.

The second live fire test of the new AIM120D-3 missile incorporating upgraded hardware in the guidance section took place over the Point Mugu Sea Test Range in California on May 12, 2021. The instrumented test vehicle was launched from F/A-18F Super Hornet BuNo 166450/DD217 assigned to Air Test and Evaluation Squadron 31 (VX-31) 'Dust Devils' based at Naval Air Weapons Station China Lake, California. The first shot took place on December 9, 2020. **Naval Air Systems Command**

ORDNANCE

Based on OPTEVOR's report released in June 2017 providing operationally relevant observations of AARGM Block 1 performance during the FOT&E and developmental test assist periods, the US Navy fielded Block 1 software and began retrofitting Block 1 software into all Block 0 AARGM missiles in July 2017. Fielding was executed without completion of operational testing and without adequately addressing the performance and software stability problems discovered during Block 1 FOT&E. To overcome the non-executed aspects of the programme, the US Navy entered contract negotiations with Orbital-Alliant Techsystems to address the overall system reliability shortfalls.

AGM-88G AARGM-ER
The US Navy's FY2016 budget included funding for the AGM-88G AARGM-ER that uses the electronics and software of the existing guidance and control sections of the AGM-88E AAGRM.

AARGM-ER's guidance system feeds from GPS, INS and the millimetre wave radar enabling combined modes of targeting. AARGM-ER is a networked weapon meaning the launch aircraft can fire the missile without any target details, instead the missile being reliant on information fed over the network from other aircraft or upon its autonomous target detection and categorisation capability, even if the target system stops emitting any signals.

New to the AAGRM-ER are an increased fuselage diameter, a modular payload section which houses the warhead and fuse, a new solid rocket motor to increase range with a new ignition safety device, and a new control actuation system with fins. At the time, the development funding was expected to last until 2020.

Development of the AARGM-ER began in January 2018.

The missile features a new fuselage configuration (with a thermal sleeve designed to minimise infrared detection) to meet the range, countermeasure resistance, and the ability to fit inside the weapons bay of the F-35C Lightning II. AARGM-ER's greater range, facilitated by the new propulsion system, enables Super Hornet and Growler launch aircraft to launch the missile from outside of a threat missile's engagement zone and strike the required target.

The missile's new profile is designed for greater manoeuvrability which is supported by placing the control section and control fins at the aft of the fuselage.

Air Test and Evaluation Squadron 23 (VX-23) based at Naval Air Station Patuxent River, Maryland conducted the first captive carriage flight using an AARGM-ER test vehicle on April 22, 2021. The flight involved a series of aerial manoeuvres to achieve the required test points to prove carriage compatibility on a Super Hornet aircraft, which was followed by the first release of a separation test vehicle (STV) in May 2021. This was the first time an AARGM-ER STV had demonstrated the ability to communicate with a launch aircraft, which then used its avionics to perform controlled free flight.

The first AARGM-ER live-fire test took place on July 19, 2021, over the Point Mugu Sea Test Range. Launch aircraft was F/A-18F Super Hornet BuNo 165832/SD122. Typical for a first weapon release, the test will have evaluated the missile's safe separation from the aircraft, its propulsion system, communication between aircraft and missile, and its range capability. It was the first in a series of weapon separation tests.

Milestone C approval was gained for the AARGM-ER on August 23, 2021, at the end of the engineering and manufacturing development (EMD) phase enabling the first low-rate initial production contract award. The EMD phase started after NAVAIR awarded Northrop Grumman Corporation a US$322.5m contract in March 2019 followed by its critical design review in February 2020, with its initial baseline design completed in April 2020.

Live fire flight testing is scheduled to continue in 2022, with initial operational capability currently planned for 2023.

AGM-154C Joint Stand-Off Weapon
The AGM-154C Joint Stand-Off Weapon (JSOW) is an autonomous, low-observable, 1,000lb-class, GPS/INS-guided air-to-ground glide weapon.

Dubbed a standoff outside point defence missile, the AGM-154 family has common airframe and common avionics that provide a modular payload assembly.

Its main components are a nose cone which houses guidance equipment, a mid-section housing the payload assembly, foldback wings, an aft section assembly housing two batteries, and an aft control section hosting four control fins.

JSOW provides an all-weather, day-night, launch and leave, standoff capability armed with a penetrator warhead.

The AGM-154C is armed with a 500lb blast fragmentation/penetrator warhead, and fitted with an uncooled, long-wave imaging infrared seeker with autonomous target acquisition algorithms for precise targeting.

AGM-154C underwent development testing with Air Test and Evaluation Squadron 31 (VX-31) at China Lake, gained approval for full-rate production in December 2004, and reached initial operating capability in the fleet in February 2005.

The latest variant, the JSOW AGM-154C-1, is the US Navy's first air-to-ground network-enabled weapon capable of attacking stationary land and moving maritime targets. It is equipped with GPS/INS-guidance, terminal IR seeker and a Link-16 data link. Integration of the Link-16 data link and updated seeker software algorithms provide capability to strike at-sea moving/relocatable targets.

JSOW C-1 began procurement in FY 2011. The AGM-154C-1 achieved IOC in June 2016. Domestic production for all variants of JSOW ended in 2017.

Dimensions: Length 158in, diameter up to 16in
Rack: BRU-32 ejector unit assembly or BRU-57 smart bomb rack

Laser-Guided Bombs
GBU-10
A 2,000lb-class laser-guided bomb (LGB) that uses either a Mk84 or BLU-117 warhead. Folding wings open upon release. BLU is a Bomb Live Unit.

Dimensions: Length 169.9in, diameter 18in

The first Block III Super Hornet, BuNo 169973, taxies out to the runway at St Louis Lambert Field for its delivery flight to Naval Air Station Patuxent River, Maryland. *Boeing*

Boeing delivered the first Block III Super Hornet, BuNo 169973, to Naval Air Systems Command in late September 2021. The aircraft is shown on take-off from St Louis Lambert Field where Boeing's F/A-18 production facility is located. **Boeing**

GBU-12
A 500lb-class LGB that uses the Mk82 or BLU-111 warhead. Folding wings open upon release.
Dimensions: Length 131in, diameter 10.7in

GBU-12F/B
A 500lb-class LGB fitted with a GPS/INS guidance kit comprising a computer control, adapter, and airfoil.
Dimensions: Length 131in, diameter 10.7in

GBU-16
A 1,000lb-class LGB that uses a Mk83 or BLU-110 warhead and a Paveway II laser guidance kit.
Dimensions: Length 144.8in, diameter 18in

GBU-24
A 2,000lb-class low-level LGB with a guidance and control, airfoil, adapter, fuse and either a BLU-109 or BLU-116 warhead.
Dimensions: Length 169.9in, diameter 14.5in

GBU-51
A 500lb-class LGB with a computer control, adapter, and airfoil, and a BLU-126 warhead.
Dimensions: Length 131.1in, diameter 10.75in

Joint Direct Attack Munition Series
GBU-31 JDAM
A 2,000lb-class GPS/INS-guided munition with a guidance tail kit fitted to a Mk84, BLU-109 or BLU-117 warhead.
Dimensions: Length BLU-109 148.6in; Mk84 or BLU-117 152.7in, diameter 25in

GBU-32 JDAM
A 1,000lb-class GPS/INS-guided munition with a guidance tail kit fitted to a Mk83 or BLU-110 warhead.
Dimensions: Length 119.6in, diameter 19.6in

GBU-38 JDAM
A 500lb-class GPS/INS-guided munition with a guidance tail kit fitted to a Mk82, BLU-111 or BLU-126 warhead.
Dimensions: Length 95.2in, diameter 17in

Due to the requirement for reduced collateral damage during the battle to retake the Iraqi city of Fallujah in November 2004, VX-31 completed accelerated development testing of the GBU-38 500lb JDAM to support fleet introduction on the Super Hornet. The 500lb-class weapon offers the lowest probability of collateral damage of all the JDAM variants. GBU-38 was not due to be integrated on Super Hornets until the introduction of software H4E.

Reflecting the urgency given to introducing the GBU-38 to the fleet, weapon separation testing commenced at NAS Patuxent River with VX-23 in January 2005. VX-31 commenced full development testing of the GBU-38 in late February 2005. The GBU-38 gained flight clearance on the Super Hornet in October 2005 using H2E+ software.

JDAM is a coordinate dependent weapon. To facilitate easier transfer of coordinates between sensors in the battle space and JDAM weapons, NAVAIR has embarked on a programme to support real time targeting via the MIDS.

MIDS was originally implemented on the Super Hornet to support the air-to-air mission. An upgrade to MIDS removed error sources associated with passing coordinates via Link-16. Used with software release H2E+ upward allows unlimited sharing of coordinates between the sensor and the shooter.

Selected Availability Anti-Spoofing Module (SAASM) is a further capability integrated into the JDAM weapon. Testing of SAASM weapons on the Super Hornet commenced in January 2005, fleet entry occurred in the summer of 2006.

This all-missile payload on VX-23's F/A-18F BuNo 165167/SD217, comprising eight inert AIM-120 AMRAAMs (on double rack LAU-127E launchers on each mid-board pylon), two inert AIM-9Ms (one on each wing-tip rail) and one inert AGM-88 HARM missile on each outer pylon, loaded for a captive carriage test flight. **Naval Air Systems Command**

ORDNANCE

F/A-18F BuNo 165170/SD222 assigned to VX-23 loaded with two 500lb-class GBU-38 instrumented test articles during iterative captive carriage trials which built up to a payload of eight munitions. **Naval Air Systems Command**

GBU-54 LJDAM
A 500lb-class GBU-38 JDAM fitted with a precision laser guidance set (a passive laser seeker) giving the weapon optional laser guidance in addition to GPS/INS.

Super Hornet Operational Test
Air Test and Evaluation Squadron 9 (VX-9) 'Vampires' based at Naval Air Weapons Station China Lake, is the operational test unit for the Super Hornet. The squadron continues to evaluate the type to prove the effectiveness of the aircraft, its systems, and weapons under operational conditions. Testing covers safety, maintainability, availability, reliability, training systems, documentation, and security.

Operational test results are entered into a test report with a recommendation. That report is received by the Air Warfare Requirements Office and is used for operational requirement documentation used for procurement decisions and release to the fleet.

VX-9 undertakes Initial Operational Test and Evaluation (IOT&E) and makes operational assessments for early buy-decisions. In 2004, VX-9 completed a 12-flight test programme for the APG-79 AESA radar.

OPEVAL (Operational Evaluation), the formal test of a fleet representative version of an aircraft, system or weapon is based on the requirements that the aircraft, system, or weapon is supposed to meet. The findings made during OPEVAL are given in the official test report.

The Super Hornet entered OPEVAL with VX-9 on May 27, 1999. The squadron used seven production Super Hornets - three F/A-18Es and four F/A-18Fs - 14 pilots and eight weapon systems officers to fly over seven hundred missions.

During a two-week detachment to Naval Air Station Key West, Florida, in June 1999, the first undertaken as part of OPEVAL, VX-9 evaluated the aircraft's tactical capability. The second detachment was spent aboard the USS *John C Stennis* (CVN 74) with VX-9 Super Hornets and personnel embarked as part of Carrier Air Wing 9 (CVW-9) to fully replicate operational carrier scenarios for OPEVAL.

In August 1999, VX-9 participated in Exercise Red Flag at Nellis Air Force Base, Nevada, to fly interdiction, fighter escort and suppression of enemy air defence missions with the Super Hornet.

During September and October OPEVAL missions assessed the aircraft's survivability against a range of real, rather than simulated, threat emitters on the China Lake range.

VX-9 completed OPEVAL on November 16, 1999. On February 15, 2000, the US Navy's Operational Test and Evaluation Force declared the Super Hornet as operationally effective and suitable.

VX-9 continues to fly the Super Hornet for FOT&E (Follow on Test & Evaluation) covering improvements or fixes to systems. The Super Hornet entered FOT&E in the third quarter of 2004.

In early 2007 under FOT&E, VX-9 worked on the Block 2 ATFLIR equipped with a data link, Block 2 SHARP equipped with a near real-time data link, IDECM and the ALE-55 Fibre Optic Towed Decoy.

The APG-79 AESA radar completed OPEVAL at the end of November 2006 using H3 software with rear-cockpit JHMCS and ACS. Two detachments were made as part of the APG-79 OPEVAL, Naval Air Station Key West, Florida, for air-to-air and Naval Air Station Fallon, Nevada, for air-to-ground.

During APG-79 OPEVAL, AESA-equipped aircraft were already assigned to the first operational squadron, Strike Fighter Squadron 213 (VFA-213) 'Black Lions'. VFA-213 held trusted agent status to VX-9 during the OPEVAL period. This allowed VFA-213 personnel to provide day-to-day flight operation data to VX-9 operational test directors for processing and inclusion into the official test findings.

Testing undertaken by VX-9 has various stages depending on where the programme is positioned in its journey to being fielded with the fleet. These are initial (IOT&E), operational (OT&E) and follow-on (FOT&E).

Between October 2008 and May 2009, VX-9 conducted OT&E of the AGM-154C-1 JSOW and the AGM-84K SLAM-ER. Two big events in 2010 involved IOT&E of the AGM-88E Advanced Anti-Radiation Guided Missile (AARGM) and FOT&E of the APG-79 AESA

radar. During FY2011, VX-9's big ticket item was the start of OT&E of the AIM-9X Block II air-to-air missile, a programme that continued until July 2013.

Between FY2012 and FY2014, VX-9 conducted OT&E of the SCS H8E software, followed by SCS H10 in FY2014 and FY2015.

In January 2016, VX-9 conducted the second operational assessment of the Infrared Search and Track pod, and subsequently started FOT&E of the AGM-88E AARGM (which concluded in March the following year).

When FY2017 started on October 1, VX-9 commenced the OT&E of SCS H12 software which included another phase of multi-sensor integration improvements, enhanced ALQ-218 geolocation, improvements to the communication countermeasures set, modifications of the aircrew to aircraft interfaces and displays to manage aircrew workload, and additional capabilities required to operate the Super Hornet in ATC-controlled airspace.

By 2019, SCS H14 was placed in OT&E with VX-9. This software suite includes more capabilities for the IRST pod and Naval Integrated Fire Control, ADS-B, UHF satellite communication, the AGM-158C Long Range Anti-Ship Missile, the 2,000lb-class Laser Joint Direct Attack Munition with a BLU-109 warhead fitted with a precision laser guidance set (a passive laser seeker) giving the weapon optional laser guidance in addition to GPS/INS, and an upgrade of the APG-79 AESA radar.

Following the standard tempo of H-series software suites entering OT&E, VX-9 started 2021 with SCS H16 on its books. H16 introduces improvements to APG-79 electronic protection, NIFC, net-enabled weapons, the IDECM suite, the mission planning system, and Block II IRST integration.

Block II Super Hornet

Raytheon ceased production of the original Super Hornet APG-73 radar in February 2006 and commenced full-rate production of the APG-79 AESA replacement. All 42 Lot 30 Super Hornets (Block II aircraft) are equipped with the APG-79, the first entire Lot to have the AESA radar. Lot 30 was also the first batch of aircraft equipped with the Raytheon ALR-67(V)3 digitally-queued radar warning receiver.

Integration of the ALR-67(V)3 and APG-79 radar gives Super Hornet a long-range ESM (electronic surveillance measures) capability. The objective is to enable a Super Hornet to be tasked on ESM missions, capable of capturing data with the ALR-67 and APG-79 and recording the information to the mission card. This allows easy data transfer to the joint mission planning system and update of the electronic order of battle.

Combat identification capability (a means of identification designed for air, land, and sea assets) were subsequently added to the Super Hornet.

In late 2006, VX-9 performed OPEVAL of an upgraded survivability package comprising the ALQ-214 jammer integrated with the ALE-55 digital (fibre) optic towed decoy.

Three years earlier, NAVAIR funded a programme to upgrade the Super Hornet's advanced mission computer to increase data throughput capacity to and from the aircraft for network-centric operations as part of the Super Hornet and Growler flight-plan.

Sensor integration combined with increased processing enables a Block II Super Hornet equipped with IDECM and the ALQ-218 ECM jammer to transmit data via the APG-79 radar for the electronic attack role.

Further development involved integrating the precision targeting workstation (PTWS) into the aircraft. PTWS overlays imagery stored in its database with imagery captured by the ATFLIR and generates an accurate target coordinate, much more quickly than the current mode of operation.

This concept enables image correlation targeting with Blue Force Tracker which is a GPS embedded system that gives commanders and troops in the field a real-time picture of the battlefield designed to improve situational awareness and reduce the possibility of friendly fire incidents. This fast air-to-ground combat ID allows multiple ground targets to be

ORDNANCE

F/A-18E BuNo 165165/SD402 assigned to Air Test and Evaluation Squadron 23 (VX-23) loaded with Mk83 general purpose bomb test articles. **Naval Air Systems Command**

tracked with either AESA or ATFLIR in all weathers.

Airborne networking was an upgrade from MIDS to JTRS (Joint Tactical Radio System - pronounced 'jitters') compatible MIDS boxes. It allows enormous quantities of data such as ground moving target indicators and combat ID overlaid on a SAR map image to be linked to and from the aircraft in milliseconds through TTNT (tactical targeting network technologies). The concept was designed to gain information superiority in the battle space and hit targets quicker and with more precision.

The performance of the APG-79 AESA radar is essential for these capabilities, for which an iterative upgrade process was implemented.

Continued Production

Department of Defense plans called for the end of domestic funding for the Super Hornet production line after FY2017. However, the plan changed because brand-new F-35Cs are entering service late and the US Navy's Super Hornet fleet has already flown more than 45% of its 6,000-hour service life. According to the US Navy's director of air warfare at the time, Rear Admiral DeWolfe Miller, the US Navy has committed to focus on F/A-18 readiness issues to keep the naval aviation force viable. This includes, sustaining the F/A-18 Hornet fleet for the US Marine Corps and US Navy Reserves, buying more F/A-18 Super Hornets to equip US Navy strike fighter squadrons, and funding

of the Service Life Modification Program (SLMP) designed to further extend the lives of most Super Hornets in the fleet and upgrade their capability.

When considering a new way of operations that is more effective, the US Navy is committed to having its major platforms on the network. The Block III upgrade is the way for Super Hornets to participate in the new way of operations and become more effective.

The US Navy's 2016 vision statement spells it out: "Naval Integrated Fire Control-Counter Air [NIFC-CA] increases the lethal range of the carrier strike group by networking otherwise individual platforms, weapons and sensors to work as one. This system-of-systems environment consists of three kill chains: from the air, from the sea and from the land. By 2025, from the air will, at a minimum, consist of the F-35B and F-35C Lightning II, the F/A-18E and F/A-18F Super Hornet, the E-2D Advanced Hawkeye, the EA-18G Growler, the multifunctional information distribution system and the AIM-120 AMRAAM missile. NIFC-CA's efforts bring the following benefits: long-range fire control and projection; the ability to operate in and control contested battlespace; and high situational awareness."

The US Navy's five-year defence plan FY2018–2022 included more than US$7bn earmarked for 80 additional Super Hornets. The President's budget in FY2018 included 14 Super Hornets and Congress added 10, 23 in

FY2019, but increased to 24 in FY2020, 14 in FY2021 and 15 in FY2022. The FY2018 request also included US$265m for development of Super Hornet Block III systems and funding for the SLMP.

Block III

Back in 2018, Captain David Kindley, the then F/A-18 programme manager with PMA-265 told the author: "Consider the Block III upgrade as four engineering change proposals: displays, networking capability, low observable configuration and a 10,000-hour service life.

"We go from the five-inch displays to 18-inch touchscreens. This has several benefits. One area not often focused on is weight reduction. When the avionic guys take out the old five-inch displays they are nearly 3ft long [they extend behind the console by 3ft] and heavy. The new displays reduce weight by about 70lb. Also, the glass in the old displays is obsolete and it is challenging getting replacements. So, we have the weight, obsolescence, logistics of the old five-inch displays, and we need the new technology displays to pass more information. What we are trying to achieve with the Block III is to improve network connectivity with the EA-18 Growler, E-2D Advanced Hawkeye, F-35 Lightning II, and ships. The future is data. We can send the data, but can the pilot and aircrew understand what they are looking at?

"Distributed Targeting Process Network [DTPN] is already a programme of record on

Super Hornet

Designed as an evolutionary upgrade of the F/A-18 Hornet, the Super Hornet first flew in 1995. The US Navy planned to buy 480 and later 565 to perform fighter, strike, and aerial refuelling roles. The aircraft replaced the F-14 Tomcat, F/A-18 Hornet and S-3 Viking (as a tanker) for operations on aircraft carriers.

Compared to the classic F/A-18 Hornet, the Super Hornet is a larger aircraft with more powerful engines, larger internal and external fuel capacity, two more weapons stations, improved avionics, and features designed to reduce the radar cross-section.

From the start of its design process, the Super Hornet was developed to incorporate new systems, sensors, and weapons continuously, following a planned update programme dubbed its roadmap. The first 178 F/A-18E and F/A-18F aircraft built in production Lots 21 to 25 are known as Block I Super Hornets (Lots 1 to 24 were F/A-18 Hornets). Block I aircraft are equipped with the Raytheon APG-73 mechanically scanned array radar and a configuration of systems like the final versions of the classic F/A-18C and F/A-18D Hornet.

In 2006, the first advanced Block II Super Hornets began to enter service equipped with the Raytheon APG-79 active electronically scanned array radar, ALQ-214 integrated defensive electronic countermeasures suite, joint helmet-mounted cueing system, Raytheon ASQ-228 ATFLIR multispectral targeting pod, Link-16 datalink, upgraded systems and new weapons. Block II was a major upgrade of the Super Hornet.

The Super Hornet roadmap updates the aircraft's high-order language or H-series system configuration software (SCS), and adds new weapons, systems, and capabilities every two years. For example, the current H14 software load introduced NIFC-CA architecture, automatic dependent surveillance-broadcast transponder dubbed ADS-B, ultrahigh frequency satellite communication, AGM-158C Long Range Anti-Ship Missile (LRASM), BLU-109 Laser Joint Direct Attack Munition hardened penetrator, and an upgrade of the APG-79 active electronically scanned array radar to keep the Super Hornet combat ready.

US Navy Super Hornets have flown in combat over Afghanistan, Iraq, and other combat theatres with glowing reports, including the 2017 shoot-down of a Syrian Air Force Su-22.

To date, Boeing has been awarded two export contracts for the Super Hornet; the Royal Australian Air Force operates 24 Block II aircraft which undertook combat operations against so-called Islamic State (IS), and the Kuwait Air Force has an order for 22 single-seat F/A-18E and six two-seat F/A-18F aircraft.

Strike Fighter Options

In 2018, Naval Air Systems Command's then PMA-265 F/A-18 and EA-18G program manager, Captain David Kindley told the author: "The US Navy has a number in mind of how many strike fighters it needs to meet mission tasking. The US Navy can adjust four levers to meet its strike fighter goal. One, buy the F-35C, the US Navy is starting to procure more Lightning IIs. Two, extend the service life of its existing Super Hornets. We are using our Super Hornets at a high rate, so we need to extend the life of the aircraft in the fleet even if we are successful in pulling all the other levers. Three, buy more Super Hornets. This makes sense in the short term, as we get a lot of capability for a reduced cost. Super Hornet is a proven platform and provides exceptionally good capability to the fleet. The problem [with this option] is that by the 2030+ timeframe they will be at the end of

F/A-18E BuNo 165779/SD401 assigned to Air Test and Evaluation Squadron 23 (VX-23) loaded for a captive carriage test flight with four inert 2,000lb-class GBU-24s and two inert AGM-88 HARM missiles. **Naval Air Systems Command**

F/A-18E BuNo 165537/SD400 assigned to Air Test and Evaluation Squadron 23 (VX-23) loaded with four 1,000lb GBU-16 instrumented test articles. **Naval Air Systems Command**

their service lives. That is why we need the Super Hornet Block III upgrade, the F-35C and to start a follow-on capability. Four, use our Super Hornets less. The US Navy is doing live virtual training and undertaking other efforts to reduce the utilisation rate on the jets.

"We have looked at many plans: the impact of new procurement, upgrades and what the Super Hornet configuration should be to complement the F-35 and achieve interoperability to meet the projected threats over the next two decades."

Existing Jets, New Jets

The author asked Captain Kindley about the earlier Block I Super Hornets. He replied: "Since the Block I forward fuselage is different to a Block II, it does not seem feasible to retrofit the Block II radar and Block III systems into a Block I aircraft. That said, Block I aircraft still have value, and we plan to use them for many years. They will be flown for training, test, adversaries, and for other uses.

"We only plan to put Block II Super Hornets through the SLMP. The US Navy's message to me is to make sure we continue to have many options to maintain our strike fighter force."

Boeing and its industry team have long funded research and flight testing of advanced Super Hornet systems. Dan Gillian, Boeing vice president, F/A-18 and EA-18G programmes, told the author: "The Block III story is different from that of the Advanced Super Hornet demonstration, which focused on stealth. The US Navy looked at the carrier air wing and its capability gaps; the Block III Super Hornet is the result of that analysis. Future fighters must be networked and survivable. Block III is about how we make the Super Hornet a networked and survivable strike fighter, one that works in a complementary way with the F-35, the EA-18G Growler and E-2D Advanced Hawkeye well into the 2040s."

Single-seat F/A-18E and two-seat F/A-18F Super Hornets equip more than 30 US Navy strike fighter squadrons, representing nearly all the tactical fighter force assigned to the nine current carrier air wings. The US Navy's long-term plan is for Block II, Block III, and Growler to make up most of the carrier air wing force structure well beyond 2035. **Lon Nordeen**

VX-23: Block III Super Hornet

The first Block III F/A-18 Super Hornet jets arrived at Air Test and Evaluation Squadron 23 (VX-23) 'Salty Dogs' in June 2020: single-seat F/A-18E (E323) and two-seat F/A-18F (F287). In October 2021, both aircraft were flying with VX-31 at China Lake conducting software functionality and networking test programmes.

Aircraft E323 and F287 are the first two. Subsequent production aircraft are expected off the Boeing production line in September and will continue at a rate of approximately two per month until contract completion in early FY2025.

As more Block III jets come off the production line, they will deliver to VX squadrons to complete the developmental and operational test phases.

In March 2019, NAVAIR awarded Boeing a US$4bn multiyear procurement contract enabling the US Navy to order a minimum of 24 Block III jets each year through FY2021. According to PMA-265, the first deployment of a Block III-equipped squadron is anticipated in mid-2023, with a plan to have two Block III-equipped squadrons (comprising new production Block IIIs and upgraded Block IIs to SLMP configuration) in each carrier air wing by 2027.

Before any deployment takes place, PMA-265's initial goal is to complete a transition from flight testing to fleet operations sometime in Q2 or Q3 of FY2022, allowing the first squadron a minimum nine-month work-up period.

Because the Super Hornet is a mature airframe, the Block III does not necessitate an extensive flight test programme. Most of the changes are internal so the set of test points is less extensive.

Lieutenant Jonathon Malycke is a test pilot assigned to VX-23 with experience of test flying the Block III aircraft.

Describing the Block III, Lt Malycke said the cockpit is completely touchscreen and completely colour, like using a big tablet. He said: "The pilot vehicle interface makes life as easy as possible for the aircrew to use the aircraft's sensors and weapons. Data throughput

ORDNANCE

F/A-18F BuNo 165170/SD422 assigned to Air Test and Evaluation Squadron 23 (VX-23) fires an instrumented AIM-9X Sidewinder test vehicle. **Naval Air Systems Command**

on the aircraft is much higher to deal with the networking requirements. Compared to an original Block II, it is like dial up to broadband. A data fusion computer fuses and presents the most relevant information pertinent to your mission and what you need to know about threats and targets in one place. Aircrew can pick out exactly what they need and use the information as quickly and as effectively | as possible."

According to Lt Malycke, the Block III's sensor fusion computer is a much more robust model than the equivalent on a Block II. The Block III fusion computer can manage the massive amounts of data received from the advanced data links and its suite of sensors and is able to fuse and place the information on the large area display (LAD).

During one of the first phases of developmental testing at Pax River, Lt Malycke put the Block III through its paces, going as fast as possible, pulling as many Gs as possible to make sure the vibrations were not going to break the LAD and the new head-up display (HUD), and were compatible with all manoeuvres within the aircraft's envelope. Other missions involved shooting the gun to check that the vibration generated by the recoil did not affect or break either the LAD or HUD.

Discussing the LAD, Lt Malycke said: "I can set up a specific scenario with the LAD using the sensors, while the weapon system operator in the aft cockpit can concurrently conduct different roles set up on the aft cockpit's LAD.

"We can display a large map on the 8x10 screen, upon which all air contacts, and all sensor inputs can be displayed. On Block II aircraft the pilot has a 5in x 5in screen though the weapon systems operator has an 8in x 10in screen. But generally, the pilot had to guess what the weapon system operator is looking at. On the Block III, both the front and aft cockpits have the exact same display."

A carrier suitability (called shake, rattle, and roll) programme followed. Using the TC-7 catapult and MK-7 arresting gear facility at Pax, Lt Malycke flew multiple worst case catapult launches (cats) and arrested landings (traps) to make sure the LAD and the HUD remain intact, in place and work properly before and after cats and traps. All operating requirements were proven.

In August, Lt Malycke deployed to Point Mugu, California to participate in a large NAVAIR test exercise in which the two Block IIIs used the networking systems and sensor fusion with Block II Super Hornets to make sure the Block III systems are compatible with the Block IIs and all the other types of aircraft in the air wing. Block II Super Hornets, EA-18G Growlers and E-2D Hawkeyes and other types conducted relevant air-to-air missions with the Block IIIs at the heart of each mission. These were fleet-representative missions designed to verify that the Block III, flown by test pilots, is compatible with the other types. Any anomalies found will have time to be fixed ahead of Block III aircraft being assigned to the first fleet squadron.

Lt Malycke explained that all the Block IIs involved were instrumented to collect data between other Super Hornets and Growlers and the sensors involved. Engineers used the data to validate the Block III's connectivity. Operating with H16 software, fixes to any issues will be included in the follow-on H18 SCS.

There are distinct versions of H16. A Block II has a different version of H16 to a Block III, to use a slang term, 'each does different stuff under the hood'.

In the cockpit, the two versions look much the same, but the pilot's interaction is different, but according to Lt Malycke, aircrew can go from a Block II to a Block III easily.

H18 will facilitate the AGM-88G Advanced Anti-Radiation Guided Missile – Extended Range (AARGM-ER) and more incremental upgrades and improvements to the aircraft's networking and infrastructure capabilities.

PMA-242, NAVAIR's direct and time sensitive strike programme office, conducted the first AARGM-ER live-fire in July to verify aircraft to missile integration, rocket motor performance, and to start modelling and simulation validation. It received Milestone C approval for the missile on August 23, the green light for production to commence.

A sailor uses a speed wrench to load 20mm high explosive incendiary rounds into the link-less ammunition feed system of an F/A-18E Super Hornet. **US Navy**

F/A-18E BuNo 165537/SD100 assigned to Air Test and Evaluation Squadron 23 (VX-23) releases a ripple salvo of seven 1,000lb Mk83 general purpose bombs fitted with BSU-85/B fins and deployed low-drag air inflatable ballutes (small parachutes). The munitions are released in sequence from stations 8, 6, 2, 10, 3, 9 and 4. **Naval Air Systems Command**

The programme will continue captive and live fire testing through 2022 with initial operational capability declaration planned for 2023.

VX-23: F/A-18 Super Hornet

Despite the high degree of commonality between the F/A-18 Super Hornet and the EA-18G Growler, VX-23 has an independent department for each which work together for weapons and systems integrated on the Growler, especially the Next Generation Jammer.

The F/A-18 department continues its long-standing developmental test role of system configuration set (SCS) software. The department has oversight of an SCS that is under developmental test (DT), one that is at a mature phase of its DT, and one at the initial requirements stage. Currently the three H-series SCS with VX-23 are additional builds of H14 each with specific capabilities: H16 in flight testing and working and developing requirements for H18.

VX-23 collaborates regularly with its sister squadron, VX-31 based at Naval Air Weapons Station China Lake, which conducts extensive SCS testing.

In parallel, VX-23 also evaluates the interoperability aspects of the SCS with all aircraft types in carrier air wings and those flown by the US Marine Corps and US Air Force.

Weapons testing is shared between VX-23 and VX-31. All live missile shots and weapon releases are undertaken on ranges in California and over the Pacific Ocean. Back at Pax River, VX-23 tends to focus on the flight science portion of a weapon's test programme.

Northrop Grumman's AGM-88G Advanced Anti-Radiation Guided Missile – Extended Range (AARGM-ER) is a current weapons integration programme underway with VX-23 and VX-31. Tests enable validation of the weapon's functionality upon launch and targeting.

Explaining, VX-23's commander, Captain Elizabeth Somerville said: "We need to ensure the weapon comes off the aircraft cleanly it will neither impact the aircraft or any adjacent stores.

"Carrier suitability testing is another part of weapons integration work at VX-23. Does the weapon have any issue with the loads from flying throughout the tactical profile, with noise, vibrations, and flutter? And is the weapon able to survive in a deployed environment on board an aircraft carrier? We load the weapon on the aircraft and use a test profile with multiple catapult shots and multiple arrested landings using the TC-7 catapult and MK-7 arresting gear facility.

"We use an instrumented aircraft and an instrumented weapon to ensure all the imposed loads are within the tolerable levels and that the weapon or the system continues to function. Can we still turn it on, to make sure it passes all its built-in tests? Whatever validated functionality works on the ground or when airborne with the weapon attached to the aircraft, does that still function after multiple cats and traps?"

SUPER HORNET FLEET AND TRAINING SQUADRONS

Mark Ayton outlines the US Navy's Super Hornet force structure and the training squadrons assigned to the Atlantic and Pacific fleets.

A shooter directs an F/A-18F Super Hornet assigned to Strike Fighter Squadron 106 (VFA-106) 'Gladiators' aboard the aircraft carrier USS George H.W. Bush (CVN 77). **US Navy/Mass Communication Specialist Sophie Pinkham**

An F/A-18F Super Hornet assigned to the 'Gladiators' of Strike Fighter Squadron 106 (VFA-106) 'Gladiators' performs a touch and go on the flight deck of the aircraft carrier USS Gerald R. Ford (CVN 78) while underway in the Atlantic Ocean conducting carrier qualifications on January 30, 2021. **US Navy/Mass Communication Specialist Kallysta Castillo**

NAVAL AIR STATION Lemoore in California has played a major part in the operational deployment of the F/A-18 Hornet for over 25 years. Lemoore is the original home of the US Navy F/A-18 Hornet and Super Hornet. Strike Fighter Squadron 125 (VFA-125) 'Rough Raiders' established there on November 13, 1980, the first F/A-18 Hornet Fleet Replacement Squadron (FRS). In January 1999 VFA-122 'Flying Eagles', the first Super Hornet FRS also established at Lemoore. The first examples of all versions of the Hornet and Super Hornet entered service with the US Navy fleet at the California base.

Strike Fighter Wing Pacific (COMSTRKFIGHTWINGPAC)

Strike Fighter Wing Pacific (SFWP) headquartered at Naval Air Station Lemoore, California, is tasked to provide combat ready Strike Fighter Squadrons trained to conduct carrier-based, all-weather attack, fighter and support missions as required by the Pacific fleet tactical commander. Twenty Super Hornet squadrons are assigned.

Pacific Fleet Air Wings

Each of the five air wings (CVW-2, CVW-5, CVW-9, CVW-11, and CVW-17) and their respective squadrons deploy under notification from Commander Naval Air Forces (COMNAVAIRPAC) Vice Admiral Kenneth Whitesell, as tasked by Commander US Pacific Fleet (CINCPACFLT), Admiral Samuel Paparo. COMNAVAIRPAC is the direct representative of and the principal advisor to CINCPACFLT for the operation, support, and administration of naval aviation in the Pacific.

As part of the support provided to the squadrons, SFWP staff ensure each one has the correct personnel, number of aircraft, the right systems and training to meet their deployment schedule.

CSFWP has a large Aircraft Intermediate Maintenance Detachment (AIMD) with

STRIKE FIGHTER WING PACIFIC SUPER HORNET SQUADRONS

Squadron	Model	Name	Tail code	Carrier Air Wing
VFA-2	F/A-18F	Bounty Hunters	NE	CVW-2
VFA-14	F/A-18E	Tophatters	NG	CVW-9
VFA-22	F/A-18F	Fighting Redcocks	NA	CVW-17
VFA-25	F/A-18E	Fist of the Fleet	AG	CVW-7
VFA-27	F/A-18E	Royal Maces	NF	CVW-5
VFA-41	F/A-18F	Black Aces	NG	CVW-9
VFA-86	F/A-18E	Sidewinders	AG	CVW-7
VFA-94	F/A-18F	Mighty Shrikes	NA	CVW-17
VFA-102	F/A-18F	Diamondbacks	NF	CVW-5
VFA-113	F/A-18E	Stingers	NE	CVW-2
VFA-115	F/A-18E	Eagles	NF	CVW-5
VFA-122	F/A-18E and F/A-18F	Flying Eagles	NJ	Fleet Replacement Squadron
VFA-136	F/A-18E	Knighthawks	AC	CVW-3
VFA-137	F/A-18E	Kestrels	NA	CVW-17
VFA-146	F/A-18E	Blue Diamonds	NH	CVW-11
VFA-151	F/A-18E	Vigilantes	NG	CVW-9
VFA-154	F/A-18F	Black Knights	NH	CVW-11
VFA-192	F/A-18E	Golden Dragons	NE	CVW-2
VFA-195	F/A-18E	Dambusters	NF	CVW-5

Notes:
VFA-27, VFA-102, VFA-115 and VFA-195 are forward deployed at Marine Corps Air Station Iwakuni, Japan. Each CVW-assigned squadron has a standard unit establishment of 12 aircraft.

about 1,000 personnel assigned to provide intermediate level maintenance support to the squadrons. AIMD has a sea operations desk, which deploys personnel to one of the five Pacific fleet carriers to augment the intermediate level of maintenance undertaken within the air wing.

Pacific Fleet Training Unit - Flying Eagles

VFA-122 'Flying Eagles' was established at Naval Air Station Lemoore, California on January 15, 1999, as the Fleet Readiness Squadron (FRS) for Super Hornet within STRIKFIGHTWINGPAC (Strike Fighter Wing Pacific). VFA-122's safe for flight certification was achieved in May 2001.

The squadron trains all pilots, weapons system operators and maintainers to fly and maintain the aircraft. VFA-122 conducts various transition courses for different categories of pilots.

Category 1
Primary transition training for student pilots.
Category 2
Transition training, for pilots coming from a different type.
Category 3
Re-qualification for pilots returning to flight operations.
Category 4
A ten-hour familiarisation course for Landing Signals Officers.
Category 5
Tailored courses for carrier re-qualification, night vision goggles (NVG) and low altitude NVG training.
The first class started in June 2000.

F/A-18 SUPER HORNET TRAINING

Nugget Course

The Category 1 course lasts nine months, includes 80 hours and starts off with familiarisation flying learning how to fly the Super Hornet in basic flight profiles, emergency procedures, how the aircraft systems work, how to operate the radar and interpret the information to conduct an intercept. By comparison, the Category 2 lasts six months with 50 to 60 hours. The Category 1 progresses to formation flying and all-weather intercepts learning how to work the radar in an air-to-air scenario and how to employ and work basic intercept geometry against other airborne targets. That moves on to the strike phase, which is dedicated to air-to-ground, learning how to employ the aircraft, delivering dumb, laser-guided, and GPS-guided bombs at low, medium, or high altitude. The next phase is fighter weapons training which focuses on advanced air-to-air intercepts. The course concludes with carrier qualifications.

The initial familiarisation phase begins with three to four weeks of academic lectures and computer aided instruction, undertaking tutorials on all the aircraft systems; it progresses with ten simulator rides and seven familiarisation flights.

Pilots gain familiarisation of the Super Hornet characteristics by undertaking general handling, basic airways navigation and flights to different airfields. Over seven flights a student gains experience of the systems and undertakes gentle manoeuvring.

Phase 2 commences with four formation flights, two as a section (two aircraft) and two as a division (four aircraft); the fourth flight qualifies the student as safe for solo flight. The first solo flight is then flown.

The next stage introduces all weather intercepts (AWI). This involves geometry and basic air-to-air radar employment against a single target. In this case another squadron aircraft flown by an instructor. AWI consists of five simulator rides and five missions involving beyond visual range weapons employment and rudimentary manoeuvring in visual scenarios. The missions involve radar-attacks conducting intercepts with simulated missile shots in a 2 v 2 scenario.

Phase 3 (the strike phase) comprises ten simulator rides and 15 flights, some flown at night. Strike teaches students the basics of air-to-ground weapon employment. The student is graded on each attack profile. The first sorties involve basic high angle bombing, learning how to drop Mk76 practice bombs from altitudes between 15,000 and 25,000ft. Sorties evolve into multiple re-attacks on a target.

Sailors assigned to the USS Nimitz (CVN 68) prepare an F/A-18E Super Hornet assigned to the 'Flying Eagles' of Strike Fighter Squadron 122 (VFA-122) for launch from the flight deck. US Navy/Petty Officer Holly Herline

Students must then learn tactical manoeuvres: low ingress to the target and pop-up attacks rolling in to deliver a practice bomb on a target. The next stage involves dropping precision-guided munitions with simulated weapon release sorties.

Strike phase culminates with close air support (CAS). Students are tasked to strike different targets each with a required time on target and different bomb impact point, whilst having to avoid simulated threats. The training is undertaken with forward air controllers on the ground at the range.

Phase 4 is fighter weapons - an advanced air-to-air syllabus involving seven flights starting with basic fighter manoeuvring (BFM). There are no simulator rides because it requires a full 360° environment. BFM engagements are all flown within visual range flying the aircraft to its maximum performance. This exposes the student to the basics of how to fight 1 v 1 against different kinds of adversaries.

More complex beyond visual range (BVR) intercepts are flown against single and multiple groups of adversaries employing simulated AIM-9 Sidewinder and AIM-120 AMRAAM missile shots. Complexity of each mission ramps up with increased threats and awareness of the forward quarter threat employed by the bandits against the student crews

Students must defeat BVR shots made by the adversaries and then make follow on shots during the engagement. The fighter weapons phase allows the student to engage the adversary at the merge.

Course culmination ends with carrier qualification (CQ). All student pilots have previously gained a CQ in the T-45 Goshawk.

CQ preparation involves six simulator rides before starting field carrier landing practice (FCLP), a series of 20 'bounce sessions' flown at Naval Air Station Lemoore. Each session comprises between six and ten bounces. The student is critiqued on every bounce by an LSO who observes each bounce from the LSO shack at the end of the runway. In addition, throughout the course when flying with either an instructor WSO or pilot they get critiqued on each pass they make. Critique made early in the course is important to prevent the student from developing bad habits.

The CQ typically involves a three-day deployment to an aircraft carrier, during which the

Landing Signal Officers watch as an F/A-18F Super Hornet assigned to Strike Fighter Squadron 106 (VFA-106) 'Gladiators' prepares to make an arrested recovery aboard the aircraft carrier USS Harry S. Truman (CVN 75) while underway in the Atlantic Ocean. US Navy/Mass Communication Specialist Kevin Murray

Moisture builds on the leading edges of an F/A-18F Super Hornet flown by pilots assigned to Strike Fighter Squadron 122's demonstration team during a high-speed pass at Mach 0.98. **US Navy/Rusty Baker**

student pilot must achieve ten day traps and six traps at night. Graduation follows upon return to Lemoore after which the pilot is posted to a fleet squadron.

Strike Fighter Wing Atlantic (COMSTRKFIGHTWINGLANT)

Naval Air Station Oceana in Virginia is home of Strike Fighter Wing Atlantic COMSTRIK-FIGHTWINGLANT (CSFWL) commanded by a commodore, Captain Ted Ricciardella. The wing is tasked by Commander Naval Air Force Atlantic (COMNAVAIRLANT), Rear Admiral John Meier to provide combat ready strike fighter squadrons trained to conduct carrier-based, all-weather attack, fighter, and support missions.

Fifteen Super Hornet squadrons are assigned.

Atlantic Fleet Air Wings

Four carrier air wings (CVW-1, CVW-3, CVW-7, and CVW-8) and their respective squadrons deploy under notification from COMNAVAIRLANT Rear Admiral John Meier, as tasked by Commander Fleet Forces Command (CFFC), Admiral Daryl Caudle. COMNAVAIRLANT is the direct representative of and the principal advisor to CFFC for the operation, support, and administration of naval aviation in the Atlantic.

Atlantic Fleet Training Unit - Gladiators

Strike Fighter Squadron 106 (VFA-106) 'Gladiators' was established at Naval Air Station Cecil Field, Florida on April 27, 1984, as the Atlantic Fleet F/A-18 Hornet FRS. The squadron moved to Naval Air Station Oceana, Virginia, during the summer of 1999 and now serves the Atlantic Fleet as the Super Hornet FRS.

VFA-106 achieved safe for flight on Super Hornet in September 2004 and commenced operations in October with a small cadre of new instructors assigned from various fleet squadrons including VFA-122 at Naval Air Station Lemoore.

In January 2005, Strike Fighter Squadron 103 (VFA-103) 'Jolly Rogers' became the first Atlantic Fleet squadron to undertake transition to the Super Hornet with VFA-106, completing in early June 2005. The second unit, VFA-11 'Red Rippers' followed in April, achieving safe for flight in November 2005.

VFA-106 stood up its first Category 1 Super Hornet class for nugget pilots arriving from Naval Training Command in August 2005. That class finished in mid-December 2005.

Training for Different Lots

The training provided by VFA-106 and VFA-122 allows a trainee pilot or WSO to fly any Lot of Super Hornet. A pilot destined to fly AESA-equipped aircraft with a fleet squadron does not

STRIKE FIGHTER WING ATLANTIC SUPER HORNET SQUADRONS

Squadron	Model	Name	Tail code	Carrier Air Wing
VFA-11	F/A-18F	Red Rippers	AB	CVW-1
VFA-31	F/A-18E	Tomcatters	NH	CVW-11
VFA-32	F/A-18F	Swordsmen	AC	CVW-3
VFA-34	F/A-18E	Blue Blasters	AB	CVW-1
VFA-37	F/A-18E	Bulls	AJ	CVW-8
VFA-81	F/A-18E	Sunliners	AB	CVW-1
VFA-83	F/A-18E	Rampagers	AC	CVW-3
VFA-87	F/A-18E	Golden Warriors	NH	CVW-11
VFA-103	F/A-18F	Jolly Rogers	AG	CVW-7
VFA-105	F/A-18E	Gunslingers	AC	CVW-3
VFA-106	F/A-18E and F/A-18F	Gladiators	AD	Fleet Replacement Squadron
VFA-131	F/A-18E	Wildcats	AC	CVW-3
VFA-143	F/A-18E	Pukin' Dogs	AG	CVW-7
VFA-211	F/A-18E	Check Mates	AB	CVW-1
VFA-213	F/A-18F	Black Lions	AJ	CVW-8

Note: Each CVW-assigned squadron has a standard unit establishment of 12 aircraft.

need to fly a AESA-equipped jet on the course because the specific capabilities of that aircraft exceed the syllabus instructed at VFA-106 and VFA-122.

The functionality differences do present a huge training issue for the instructors who must fly in all Lots going from one to another depending on the training event.

Some Lots have different software configurations loaded, which has controller functionality issues for the WSO in the aft seat.

Some training events require a basic cockpit others require a missionised one, such as those equipped with the APG-79 AESA radar which have very different functionality characteristics.

Rear Admiral John Meier (right) commander, Naval Air Forces Atlantic, and Captain J. J. Cummings, USS Gerald R. Ford's (CVN 78) commanding officer, communicate with the pilot of an F/A-18F Super Hornet while overseeing landings from the LSO platform on the ship's flight deck. **US Navy/Mass Communication Specialist Zack Guth**

F/A-18 SUPER HORNET

SUPER HORNET RENOVATION

Lon Nordeen details Boeing's Service Life Modification Program currently underway to sustain the US Navy's Super Hornet fleet.

F/A-18F BuNo 165911/NA400 launches from one of the two bow catapults on *USS Theodore Roosevelt* (CVN 71). Dubbed a cat, a catapult launch is another high-energy flight operation endured by carrier borne aircraft. The aircraft shown is operated by Strike Fighter Squadron 94 (VFA-94) 'Mighty Shrikes' based at Naval Air Stations Lemoore, California. **US Navy/Mass Communication Specialist Alexander Corona**

VICE ADMIRAL TROY Shoemaker, then Commander Naval Air Forces, told the US House of Representatives Armed Services Committee on November 9, 2017: "The hardest hit community within naval aviation is the strike fighter community . . . at the beginning of October [2017], in our Super Hornet community alone, only half of our total inventory of 542 aircraft were flyable or mission capable, and only 170 or 31% of the total inventory were fully mission capable and ready to fight . . . This year [2017], we deployed four carrier strike groups to support combat operations and provide strategic deterrence around the world. Consistent with the Navy's policy of supporting deployed and next to deploy forces, we were forced to cannibalise aircraft, parts, and [shift] people to ensure those leaving on deployment had what they needed to be safe and effective while operating forward. To continue to provide credible maritime forces around the world, we've made sacrifices at home . . . To act on immediate readiness issues, such as low manning, long-term down aircraft, parts shortages, and lack of facilities, we established a Rhino Readiness Recovery team to identify and address long-term impacts."

The US Navy has nine carrier air wings to deploy on the ten aircraft carriers currently in service. Eight of the nine air wing includes four strike fighter squadrons (most fly Super Hornets, some deploy with one US Marine Corps Hornet unit), a squadron of helicopters plus critical support aircraft such as the E-2C or E-2D Hawkeye airborne early warning and EA-18G Growler electronic attack aircraft. US Navy Hornets are being phased out and new F-35Cs now equip the first squadron, Strike Fighter Squadron 147 (VFA-147) 'Argonauts', currently underway in the Indo-Pacific region on the stealthy jet's first deployment embarked on a super carrier.

On February 26, 2021, Strike Fighter Squadron 97 (VFA-97) 'Warhawks' ended over 30 years of service operating the F/A-18C Hornet and F/A-18E Super Hornet and began transition to the F-35C Lightning II as the US Navy's second fleet squadron operating the type. VFA-97 was expected to achieve its safe for flight status with the F-35C by January 2021.

The Navy's Super Hornet fleet needs to last since a significant percentage of the strike fighter force will be made up of these aircraft beyond 2035. In the 2030 timeframe, the US Navy's plan is to equip carrier air wings with four strike fighter squadrons, two equipped with F-35C Lightning IIs and two with Super Hornet.

Naval Air Systems Command's PMA-265 programme manager for the F/A-18 and EA-18G until July 2019, Captain David Kindley said: "The taxpayer bought a 6,000-hour airframe in the legacy Hornet and Super Hornet. With the earlier plan of procurement for the F-35, these numbers appeared fine. However, our operational tempo remained high and the IOC [initial operation capability] for a few platforms slid to the right. We were left with a challenge of keeping our flight decks filled while we work to develop and field new aircraft. This is when we started to talk about [Super Hornet] life extension."

To sustain the US Navy strike fighter force, the service is planning to buy 340 F-35C Lightning IIs, procure 90 or more new F/A-18 Super Hornets in the improved Block III configuration and extend the life of and upgrade existing Block II Super Hornets. New jets will be procured across the FYDP: 24 Block IIs in the FY2018 budget, and 110 Block IIIs in FY2019, for a total of 134 Super Hornets through to FY2023.

On March 1, 2018, the US Navy awarded Boeing a $73.2 million contract to initiate the Service Life Modification Program (SLMP) for the Super Hornet.

In December 2021, there were 33 Super Hornet-equipped strike fighter squadrons (23 operating the single-seat F/A-18E and ten with the two-seat F/A-18F), two fleet replacement squadrons (training units) and three air test and evaluation squadrons in the US Navy fleet.

Block I, Block II

The first 178 Super Hornets built were all configured to Block I standard equipped with systems similar to late model F/A-18 Hornets, including the Raytheon APG-73 radar. These aircraft continue to serve with front line US Marine Corps squadrons for many more years, others will continue to be used for training and test. Under the current plan, most Block I aircraft will not have their service life extended.

Over 300 Super Hornets built after 2005 were delivered in Block II configuration equipped with:

the Raytheon APG-79 active electronically scanned radar

an improved defensive countermeasures system featuring the Raytheon ALR-67(V)3 radar warning receiver and the BAE Systems

F/A-18 SUPER HORNET

ALQ-214(V)3 Integrated Defensive Electronic Countermeasures system comprising an ITT signals receiver, a BAE Systems onboard jamming techniques generator and the ALE-55 fibre-optic towed decoy
  upgraded mission computers
  high-order language operational flight program software
  an aft cockpit featuring an 8 x 10-inch tactical display
  new avionics
  enhanced power and cooling systems
  a fibre-optic data bus
  solid-state data recorder
  a distributed targeting system featuring an image processing module capable of comparing a synthetic aperture radar map, with maps held in a database for precise targeting of GPS-guided weapons
  the joint helmet-mounted cueing system AIM-9X Sidewinder and the AIM-120C-7 AMRAAM air-to-air missiles

Block I and Block II aircraft are upgraded on an approximate two-year cycle by updating the operational flight program software and adding new systems and weapons in accordance with a so-called road map managed by PMA-265. Current plans call for all surviving Block II aircraft to go through a service life extension program (SLEP) and upgrade to the Block III configuration. It should be noted that the SLEP is not the SLMP referred to above which includes some subsystems used in the SLEP and features upgrades to configure the aircraft to Block III standard.

Block III

Boeing's Vice President for Hornet and Super Hornet Programs Dan Gillian said: "The US Navy looked at its carrier air wings and capability gaps. The Super Hornet Block III is the result of that analysis. Future fighters [particularly the F-35C Lightning II] are networked and survivable. The Block III [configuration] is how we make a Super Hornet networked and survivable to operate in a complementary way with the F-35, the EA-18G Growler and E-2D Advanced Hawkeye as a front-line fighter well into the 2040s."

Originally the Block III configuration added five additional systems: conformal fuel tanks, an advanced cockpit, network connectivity, stealth characteristics, and a life extension programme.

In February 2018, NAVAIR awarded Boeing a $219.6 million contract to develop and integrate conformal fuel tanks on to the Super Hornet and EA-18G Growler, adding 3,200lb fuel capacity in low-drag tanks, extending the aircraft's range by 100–120 miles and increasing its mission flexibility. However, following issues encountered with performance, cost and schedule, NAVAIR issued stop-work orders to Boeing for work related to conformal fuel tanks on January 6, 2021.

The Block III will feature an advanced cockpit equipped with Elbit large flat-panel displays featuring a next-generation user interface.

To improve the Block III's network connection capability, the aircraft will feature two pieces of hardware from the EA-18G Growler, described by Dan Gilbert as "the Distributed Target Processor Network [DTPN] and Tactical Targeting Network Technology [TTNT]. DTPN is the big computer providing significant increase in computer power and adds multilevel security and open architecture. That is how new applications can be integrated to the platform faster than ever before to adapt to the future fight. The TTNT is the big pipe [a high-capacity, high-bandwidth network] for Super Hornet designed to plug into the EA-18G Growler and E-2D. It adds an ability to move a bandwidth of data back and forth between platforms, which is a key part of the future fight."

The TTNT is designed and manufactured by Rockwell Collins.

Discussing the Block III's stealth credentials, Gilbert said: "We will add a bit of stealth technology to the aircraft through coatings and treatments. Another really important upgrade is the integration of the [Lockheed Martin ASG-34] infrared search and track sensor that adds long-range counter air, counter stealth and targeting: a unique capability the Super Hornet brings to the carrier air wing."

Lastly, Gilbert said the Block III's service life will include structural updates to give a 10,000-hour airframe off the production line.

Service Life Modification Program

In 2008, the US Navy and a contractor team led by Boeing and Northrop Grumman began the Service Life Assessment Program (SLAP) to evaluate high-time Super Hornets to determine the effects of wear and corrosion and to determine possible service life extension plans.

Captain Kindley said: "There are two elements of the Super Hornet life extension from the original 6,000 to 10,000 flight hours. First, we undertook the Service Life Assessment Program, where we took a detailed look at the structure of the airplane to answer the question: what pieces and parts need to be modified and/or replaced to get to a longer life?

"We actually assessed the Super Hornet [to the point] where we could get it to fly to 12,000 flight hours. The direction we have from the Chief of Naval Operations is to go to the 9,000-flight hour level and tell us if you can go further within the bounds of affordability [Boeing and NAVAIR eventually agreed to a 10,000-hour service life].

"The Super Hornet Service Life Modification Program is way more than just a SLEP. It starts

The first two F/A-18 Super Hornets in Boeing's St Louis modification facility at the start of their service life modification programme. Boeing

F/A-18F Super Hornet BuNo 165672 (c/n F11) inside Boeing's facility at St Louis after being de-spliced in preparation for service life modification work. Boeing

F/A-18E Super Hornet BuNo 166598/AG112 takes the wire on the flight deck of the USS Dwight D Eisenhower (CVN 69). Dubbed a trap, catching the wire is one of the high-energy flight operations endured by carrier borne aircraft. The aircraft shown is operated by Strike Fighter Squadron 143 (VFA-143) 'Pukin' Dogs' based at Naval Air Stations Oceana, Virginia. US Navy/Mass Communication Specialist Nathan Parde

An F/A-18E Super Hornet assigned to Strike Fighter Squadron 113 (VFA-113) 'Stingers', launches from the flight deck of USS Theodore Roosevelt (CVN 71) in the Arabian Gulf. Saltwater, rainwater, and steam shroud the jet, conditions that exist every day while based at sea. US Navy/Mass Communication Specialist Alex Corona

with the airframe changes and then we add in capability updates. When you get a legacy Hornet from the depot today, after six to 24 months of overhaul work, the receiving squadron has three months more work to do to add upgrades to configure the aircraft for combat. This is unacceptable. Chief of Naval Operations told us at the PMA [NAVAIR's Program Manager Air], when you deliver a Super Hornet from the SLMP it will be a war fighter. When Boeing delivers a new Super Hornet Block III or an updated one from the SLMP line, within a day or two it should be able to go to war."

The first two Super Hornet to arrive at Boeing's St Louis facility, F/A-18E BuNo 166435 (c/n E80) and F/A-18F BuNo 165672 (c/n F11), were learning aircraft used to familiarise the engineers and production operatives with the work involved in the SLMP. The first aircraft to enter the SLMP arrived at St Louis on April 5, 2018.

Issues with Service Life Modification

When the SLMP was implemented, fleet squadrons were using up between 300 and 400 hours per Super Hornet aircraft per year, numbers varied from unit to unit. At the time, PMA-265 had forecast how many aircraft would reach their 6,000-flight hour limit for the following years: three or four in FY2018; seven to 10 in FY2019 and 18 or so in FY2020. These numbers formed the basis for induction into the SLMP.

Speaking to the author at the time, Captain Kindley said that PMA-265 decided to have Boeing perform the Super Hornet SLMP after considerable evaluation and for two main reasons.

At the time, the Naval Air Depots were very busy, their respective workloads were high and capacities low. Asking them to perform Super Hornet SLMP would have increased their workloads too high that they would not have been able to achieve the schedule of work. Second, PMA-265 built options into the contract with Boeing that once SLMP was in production, NAVAIR and therefore the government owned all data gathered and in the 2023 timeframe holds and option to offload some or all the SLMP work to the depots.

F/A-18 SUPER HORNET

Captain Kindley liked Boeing's response to the options. Boeing's intent is to make the SLMP contract the worst business case decision PMA-265 had ever made. Boeing's goal is to have the dollars to perform the SLMP better than having the depot do the work. Commenting, Kindley said he was excited that PMA-265 retains this option and asked Boeing to prove their ability to perform the contract to schedule.

Kindley said: "The industry SLMP decision was made based on depot capacity and a new set of engineering processes and decision-making to accomplish our goals. For example, with a legacy Hornet at the North Island depot, we open a panel and find a part that is broken and appears to be a new first-time problem. So, we make an order for replacement parts and can do little during the lead time for the parts to be delivered. This was very common with the legacy Hornet SLEP. It is one of the major reasons we have been so stressed with the legacy Hornet SLEP. "We also have engineering disposition challenges. Is the hole we see here AOK or a downer? So, let's go ask the engineers, but they are so busy the answer takes a long time to get."

Kindley pointed out that Boeing, which builds the Super Hornet, does not have the same legal and budgeting restrictions as the government depot. He said: "They can buy parts and components the SLAP showed that need to be replaced in advance. Also, if US Navy engineers are willing to give Boeing broad engineering authorisations, which is hard to argue, since they designed and build the aircraft in the same building, we can collapse most of the timelines and produce a final product faster."

Lessons from a SLEP

Captain Kindley remarked: "The legacy Hornet SLEP is not in a state of production. Nearly every Hornet is treated as a unique event. We are trying to learn lessons from airplane to airplane, but it has been an especially hard slog. There are a bunch of factors that also added to the Hornet challenge: we went from 6,000 to 8,000 hours and then tried for more. We have tried to include all the lessons learned from the legacy Hornet SLEP into the Super Hornet SLMP. A shallow multiphase ramp-up is planned to focus on learning how to move quickly and establish the SLMP in production. The run phase will be based on a fixed price, so Boeing will be turning out SLM aircraft in a production line way, and we still have the option for the depots to participate. This is different [from] the legacy Hornet, and [I] feel that if we tried to repeat what we did with the legacy Hornet SLEP, then someone should lose their job, because there were so many lessons learned from that process."

Modification Plans

Discussing the plan, Boeing's Vice-President for Hornet and Super Hornet Programs, Dan Gillian, said: "We will extend the life of the Super Hornet airframe, bring in the Block II to Block III conversion and add in the additional statement of work to make the airplane work better for the Navy. We will use a production mind set and programme to produce 30 to 50 aircraft per year. This is an industry-led effort with Boeing, Northrop Grumman, and close collaboration with PMA-265, and the Defense Contract Management Agency. The government is contracting with industry to extend the life of Super Hornets from 6,000 to 10,000 hours, add Block III systems and other mods. All of this goes to a production shift because data analytics will play a major role to make the work standard and repeatable. We know some parts of every plane will be a little different, but we will minimise the difference to maximise throughput. This is a ground-breaking initiative."

Boeing's SLMP manager, Mark Sears, commented: "We prepared Building 101 for the SLMP, bought tooling and the parts

With the arresting hook lowered, this F/A-18E Super Hornet is seen moments from an arrested landing on the flight deck of the USS George Washington (CVN 73). The hook works in conjunction with the ship's arresting gear which comprise the arresting cables; purchase cables, which connect the arresting wire to the arresting gear engines; sheaves which the purchase cables run through; and arresting engines that absorb the energies resulting from the aircraft's landing. Each arresting hook is made up of an arm, shank, and pivot, and are removed from the aircraft after 300 traps and sent for refurbishment.
US Navy/Mass Communication Specialist Seaman Apprentice Matthew Riggs

required to correct emergent conditions as encountered in the Super Hornet SLAP. The first four Super Hornets entered the programme in April 2018: two Block I and two Block II aircraft. We focused mostly on the life extension and undertook some mod work. We then worked on getting the engineering done to prepare shop floor instructions so we could move forward with the production ramp up at both the St Louis and San Antonio sites … in June 2019 the first Super Hornets arrived at the San Antonio facility. The San Antonio site has a workforce that is very experienced with modification work. Through to 2022, the SLMP is primarily focused on life extension, subsystem reset and maintenance to improve the material condition of the aircraft. We delivered the first life extension Super Hornets from the Boeing line in late 2019. When the programme was launched, not all the engineering for the life extension was complete. We learnt more as we got into the SLMP. Block III went through engineering, flight test and development during 2019, after which we developed and secured the kits and parts for the Block III update which were installed following the life extension update."

"The Service Life Modification Program is providing a critical resource for the US Navy to re-capitalise on long-serving aircraft to return them to the fleet in a near new condition. It will reduce burden on our maintainers, our supply system and our depot level assets within the enterprise."

CAPTAIN STEPHEN MAY, PMA-265

F/A-18 SUPER HORNET

An F/A-18E Super Hornet assigned to Strike Fighter Squadron 31 (VFA-31) 'Tomcatters' performs a bolter on the flight deck of USS *Gerald R Ford* (CVN 78). Dubbed bolter, the term means a touch and go, another high-energy, and routine flight operation. **US Navy/Mass Communication Specialist Ryan Carter**

First Deliveries

Boeing delivered the first F/A-18 Super Hornet to undergo the Service Life Modification Program back to the US Navy during October 2019. The second SLMP jet followed at the end of the month, and the third in April: all three were modified at its St Louis, Missouri facility.

According to Boeing, the initial Super Hornets delivered back to the US Navy under the first phase of SLMP extended the service life from 6,000 to 7,500 flight hours: jets which undergo phase 2 will be delivered with service lives extended to 10,000 hours and feature new Block III capabilities: enhanced network capability, an advanced cockpit system, signature improvements and an enhanced communication system.

Commenting on the first delivery, Captain Stephen May, PMA-265 co-lead for Super Hornet said: "The SLMP is providing a critical resource for the US Navy to re-capitalise on long-serving aircraft to return them to the fleet in a near new condition. It will reduce burden on our maintainers, our supply system and our depot level assets within the enterprise."

At the time of the delivery, 15 Super Hornets were undergoing the SLMP on Boeing's production lines at St. Louis, Missouri and San Antonio, Texas. Boeing said it took 18 months to complete the SLMP modifications on a Super Hornet which the company hoped to drive down 12 months as production line operatives become more efficient at the process.

During January 2021, the fourth Super Hornet to undergo the SLMP and the first completed at Boeing's San Antonio production line (F/A-18F BuNo 166621), was delivered back to the US Navy. As an indicator of the SLMP's production ramp-up, by early January, Boeing had 25 aircraft in SLMP production.

Commenting in the ramp-up at the time, Boeing said the San Antonio line will handle a higher portion of jets inducted into the SLMP and confirmed that EA-18G Growler aircraft are likely to undergo the SLMP. Once the SLMP is running at full-rate production, 80% of aircraft will be sent to San Antonio with the other 20% of jest going to St Louis.

A Defense Contract Management Agency Perspective

Describing the SLMP, Captain Paul Filardi of the Defense Contract Management Agency (DCMA) based with Boeing at its St Louis facility said: "The SLMP is one of the US Navy's top priority endeavours and is estimated to run for more than 15 years at a cost of approximately $7.8 billion. The SLMP operates under the philosophy, 'one program, two sites,' with SLMP activities being accomplished in two phases at two locations — St. Louis and San Antonio." The San Antonio facility is on Kelly Field, part of Lackland Air Force Base, and named the Aircraft Integrated Maintenance Operations, Kelly. Explaining the phased approach, Jess Overby, the DCMA SLMP integrator also based with Boeing at its St Louis facility said: "The first phase is an 18-month process of inspection, modification, repair and restoration that will extend the service life of the aircraft by 25% — from its current 6,000 flight hour limitation to 7,500 flight hours. During this phase, the Super Hornet aircraft will be extensively disassembled, thoroughly inspected, and undergo modification and repairs exceeding 5,000 hours at a cost of over $10 million per aircraft.

"The second phase of the program is a 12-month process of extensive modifications to the aircraft's launch system structure and components, arresting gear system and components, and

F/A-18F BuNo 166621/AD267 was the first Super Hornet to be re-delivered to the US Navy in late January 2021. The aircraft is seen under tow at Boeing's San Antonio facility. **Boeing**

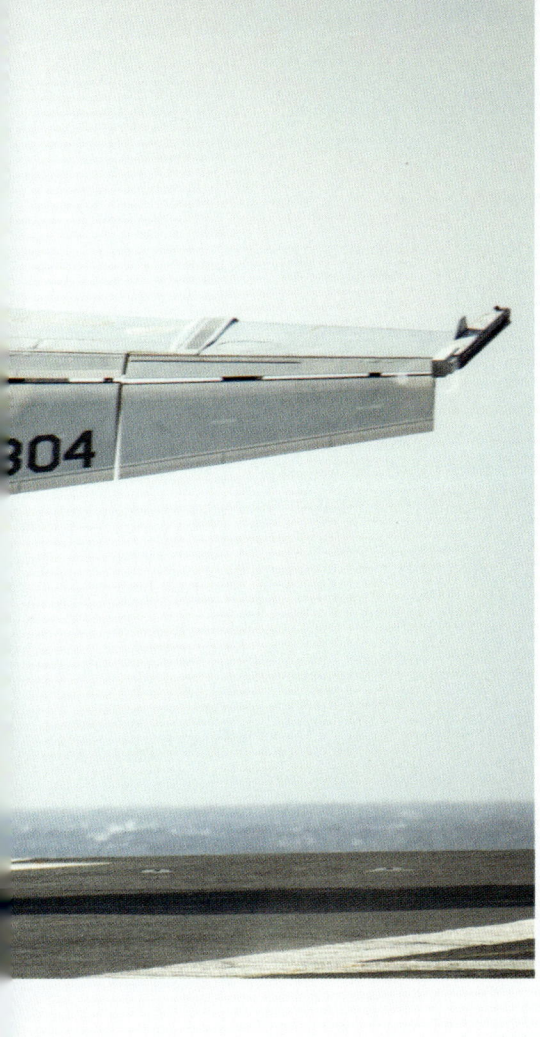

certain structural areas of the aircraft. In addition, each aircraft will get new paint. During this time the aircraft will also be ungraded with Block III capabilities."

After completion of the second phase, the aircraft life expectancy will be extended again, taking the aircraft from 7,500 to 10,000 flight hours, for a total life extension of 67% from its original 6,000 flight-hour limit and adding approximately a decade more service.

According to Captain Filardi: "The main challenge for the Super Hornet SLMP is that the condition of each aircraft is unknown. Having been operational for up to 15 years or more, the F/A-18E/F Super Hornet aircraft inducted for SLMP all have over 5,500 flight hours, thousands of take-offs, and landings, including carrier launch and recovery, and have been subjected to harsh atmospheric environments. Corrosion, stress, and fatigue damage is found on every aircraft."

Recognising the skill and effort required Jess Overby said; "Identifying, investigating, and analysing the damage, then developing disposition instructions and repairing the damage takes expert knowledge and experience, both from our industry counterparts and DCMA team members at Boeing's St Louis and San Antonio facilities."

A view of the ship's ramp (the start of the flight deck) from the cockpit of an F/A-18 Super Hornet moments from an arrested landing. **US Navy**

WWW.KEY.AERO 77

EA-18G GROWLER

BACK IN 2001, the US Department of Defense tasked the Department of the Navy to undertake an analysis of alternatives for a new-generation electronic attack aircraft.

The result of the study was the EA-18G Growler, a variant of the F/A-18F Super Hornet, built and configured as a stand-off and escort jammer for the US Navy. Now in its second decade of US Navy service, the EA-18G is the only dedicated tactical electronic attack aircraft in the Department of Defense inventory.

Captain Jason Denney, the F/A-18 Hornet and EA-18G Growler program manager with Naval Air Systems Command's PMA-265 said the aircraft has a fantastic ability to disrupt signals, deny communications, jam radars, and provide crucial support and intelligence not just to a carrier strike group, but deployed combatant commanders. He said: "The Growler's ability to work with all other aircraft, not just those in the carrier air wing but within the DoD, makes it a critical node operating with deployed Air Force, Army and Marine Corps expeditionary units; interoperability is a large key performance parameter for the Growler."

Growler

The EA-18G Growler is a carrier based electronic attack aircraft built by McDonnell Douglas Corporation, a wholly owned subsidiary of the Boeing Company.

The purpose of the airborne electronic attack (AEA) system for the EA-18G is to provide electronic surveillance and electronic attack capabilities. The AEA system incorporates an electronic attack unit as the AEA system controller, the ALQ-218(V)2 receiver system, the ALQ-227B communications countermeasures set, the Block 3 multi-mission advanced tactical terminal, and ALQ-99 jamming pods. The digital memory device and interference cancellation unit have also been added to achieve the needs of the EA-18G.

The mission of the EA–18G is the suppression of hostile search, acquisition, tracking, and guidance radar systems, and RF communications that might be employed against own-ship and other friendly (specifically the protected entity) aircraft. This mission encompasses protection of friendly aircraft as they enter and depart a battlefield region, as well as during the friendly strike aircraft mission in that battlefield region. The mission is accomplished through means of electronic attack, and/or weapon delivery, to the threat. This new mission is for the protection of multiple friendly aircraft in a multiple hostile threat environment. The electronic attack portion is accomplished via the crew vehicle interface with the AEA subsystem functionality controlled through the mission computers (MCs). This interface includes both display of threat situational awareness provided by AEA subsystem threat detection track file information processed in the MCs, and a command-and-control interface of the AEA subsystem through the MCs via options on the display formats, and cockpit hand controls that provide HOTAS (hands on throttle and stick) switches. The EA-18G employs EW tactics as offensive measures. The primary function of the EA-18G is offensive jamming.

The aircraft is powered by two GE Aviation F414-GE-400 turbofan engines using full authority digital engine control. The aircraft features a variable camber mid-wing with leading edge extensions (LEX) mounted on each side of the fuselage. Twin vertical tails are angled outboard 20° from the vertical.

The aircraft is designed with relaxed static stability to increase manoeuvrability and to reduce approach and landing speed. The aircraft is controlled by a digital fly-by-wire flight control system through hydraulically actuated flight control surfaces: ailerons, twin rudders, leading edge flaps, trailing edge flaps, LEX spoilers, and differential stabilators. The leading edge of the wing incorporates a snag, which increases outboard wing area and increases roll authority in the approach and landing configuration. The upper surface of the wing incorporates a solid wing-fold fairing cover and partial-span fence to improve transonic handling qualities at elevated angle-of-attack. A speed brake function is provided by differential deflection of the primary flight control surfaces.

The pressurised cockpit is enclosed by an electrically operated clamshell canopy. An aircraft mounted auxiliary power unit provides self-contained start capability for the engines.

System Design and Development

In late October 2006, the first System Design and Development (SDD) EA-18G Growler

A three-ship of Growlers assigned to Electronic Attack Squadron 135 (VAQ-135) 'Black Ravens' in 2012. The squadron's then CAG-bird BuNo 166941/NL521 is nearest the camera. **US Navy/Cdr Scott Janik**

BEEPS & SQUEAKS

Mark Ayton charts the development of the EA-18G Growler electronic attack aircraft.

EA-18G GROWLER

Scorpion 544 lands at Naval Air Weapons Station China Lake in California. **Paul Ridgway**

Electronic Attack Squadron 141's CAG-bird is seen catching a wire while underway in the Mediterranean. **Matthew Clements**

EA1 commenced mission systems testing in the anechoic chamber at Naval Air Station Patuxent River, Maryland. , Naval Air Station Whidbey Island, WashingtonThe EA-18G Growler is the electronic attack version of the two-seat F/A-18F Super Hornet. It is the first aircraft to be operated by the US Navy bearing the name Growler, a title which is traditionally associated with ships and submarines.

Growler SDD aircraft EA1 and EA2 made their respective maiden flights at St Louis a month earlier than planned.

Growler is a full-digital aircraft fitted with ALQ-218 and ALQ-99 systems. The analogue ALQ-99 pods used on the EA-18G have converters to enable interface with the digital platform.

An EA-18G features many of the systems integrated on a Super Hornet, including the APG-79 radar, ACS, JHMCS and weapons.

As part of the development programme, many EA-6B Prowler aircrew conducted missions in the EA-18G simulator to provide suggestions on improvements and feedback in respect of the human-system interface. This helped to overcome concerns about switching the electronic attack mission from the Prowler with four crew to a two-man Growler.

Increased automation – autopilot functions that allow the pilot to set-up the aircraft before take-off, mission computer processing power and better algorithms - help to mitigate the workload for a two-man aircrew. Workload has been divided into two in the Growler. This means the pilot is much more involved with the airborne electronic attack mission – making pilot-EWO co-ordination critical for mission success. But despite the level of automation afforded by the aircraft, the workload remains "intense but manageable", according to one Growler pilot.

Much of the tactical mission information once displayed in the aft cockpit of the EA-6B Prowler displays in the forward cockpit of the EA-18G. Thanks to ACS, Growler aircrew can select what they need to see on their individual displays. Pilot involvement in the tactical aspects of the mission and pilot-WSO coordination is critical for mission success of the EA-18G.

From an operating perspective, the EA-18G carries slightly more fuel than the Prowler and has four more stations - two more wing stations to carry AGM-88 HARMs and two cheek stations for carriage of the AIM-120 AMRAAM.

A typical EA-18G load-out for the initial Block 1 configured aircraft was three ALQ-99 pods, two AGM-88 HARMs, two AIM-120 AMRAAMs and two drop tanks, with a launch weight of 66,000lb. The initial configuration was from the early days of the Grower programme, today load-outs in fleet aircraft change to meet mission requirements.

Testing

In April 2007, the director, operational test, and evaluation, reported that the demonstrated maturity of the Growler's mission capabilities had exceeded planned expectations for the stage of system development at the time. Naval Air Systems Command's Air Test and Evaluation

An EA-18G Growler lands aboard the flight deck of the aircraft carrier USS *George Washington* (CVN 73) back in 2012, when the *Washington* was America's forward-deployed carrier, homeported at Yokosuka, Japan. **US Navy/Mass Communication Specialist 3rd Class William Pittman**

VAQ-139's CAG-bird EA-18G Growler BuNo 168256/NA500 seen landing at Naval Air Station Fallon, Nevada. **Dan Stijovich**

Squadron 23 (VX-23) 'Salty Dogs' based at Patuxent River conducted 11 flight test missions that successfully demonstrated the EA-18G's end-to-end capability, including the crew interaction, to detect, identify, and jam simple threats in-flight.

Based on the first successful operational assessment (OA), the Milestone Decision Authority and the undersecretary of defense for acquisition, technology, and logistics approved entry into the EA-18G LRIP for the first phase (eight kits) of the 26 total planned LRIP EA-18G Airborne Electronic Attack (AEA) kits.

Development Testing (DT) transitioned from the anechoic chamber to flight test at Patuxent River with EA1 and EA2 using the test ranges and simulated emitters available there. The DT effort then moved to Naval Air Weapons Station China Lake to develop employment tactics using real emitters on the China Lake range. The EA-18G DT test effort was shared between VX-23 based at Patuxent River and VX-31 based at China Lake.

Developmental Flight Test

The Growler flight test programme was split between aeromechanical and mission system phases. In July 2004, NAVAIR dedicated three aircraft to the programme.

F/A-18E E3 BuNo 165167
Carrier suitability and flight loads
F/A-18E E22 BuNo 165779
Flutter
F/A-18F F35 BuNo 165875
Flying qualities and performance

All three Super Hornets were modified to represent G-model aircraft fitted with wing tip pods and other sub-systems with the same weight, centre of gravity and aerodynamic characteristics. F/A-18F F35 commenced flying as such on March 30, 2006.

VX-23 undertook 346 flights for the test programme comprising 109 flutter, two flying qualities, 46 noise and vibration, 80 loads, 97 flying qualities and performance and 14 weapon separations (WSEP).

F/A-18E E10 BuNo 165537/SD100 was instrumented for WSEP and conducted Growler separation trials and ALQ-99 testing.

F35, the only two-seat aircraft involved, received a full set of EA-18G components comprising a series of fuselage antennas, a blade antenna on top of the fuselage for the Multi-mission Advanced Tactical Terminal, antennas on the aft underside near the horizontal stabilisers for the ALQ-218 receiver, bumps, fences and ALQ-218 wing-tip pods. All were easily distinguishable and coloured orange, the standard colour used for test equipment.

The ALQ-218 wing-tip pods created significant changes to the wing's aerodynamic and moment of inertia. Both conditions impacted on the flutter testing more than anything else and were in addition to the effects created by heavy ALQ-99 pods loaded under the wing.

F/A-18F F35 also received what's known as a fence on the top of the wing, known as the TFQI or transonic flying qualities improvement (TFQI). The fences were fitted to improve the aircraft's flying qualities at transonic speeds, especially when carrying a heavy load typical for a Growler.

Aeromechanical Phase

The aeromechanical phase comprised seven main test programmes: flying qualities, performance (covering take-off and climb), flutter (covering full subsonic and supersonic flutter programmes), carrier or CVS demonstration, flight loads, several phases of the noise and vibration survey (one with E3 and one with G1) and ALQ-99 safe separation.

F/A-18F F35 commenced flying as a G-configured aircraft on March 30, 2006, beginning a 350-flight, 20-month aeromechanical flight test phase. Aircraft F35 was used to expand the flying envelope and performance test points during the 97-flight flying qualities and performance component.

The aircraft also performed source error correction tests for the pitot static system fitted to the aircraft's slightly re-profiled radome. F35 also performed testing of the automated carrier landing system, and the newer precision approach landing system.

In the first week of April 2006, aircraft E22 joined the test programme. For the first year or so, E22 was connected to hydraulic rams for ground-based dynamic flutter testing after which it commenced a 106-flight flutter programme.

And later that month, aircraft E3 started an 80-flight loads test programme involving what US Navy test pilots called 'up and away' loads with

EA-18G BuNo 168376/NG500, VAQ-133's CAG-bird, moments from launch from a catapult of the aircraft carrier USS *John C Stennis* (CVN 74) during its 2017 deployment. **US Navy/VAQ-133**

full-on g-loads. E3 was also used for carrier loads testing at Patuxent River. Using Pax River's MK-7 arresting gear, the aircraft made 17 traps (arrested-landings) and five cats (catapult launches) loaded with various weights (comprising ALQ-99 pods and an AGM-88 HARM missile) up to the Growler's maximum of 48,000lb.

Fully-instrumented, aircraft E3 was also used to conduct an initial survey of the noise and vibration environment encountered by ALQ-99 jamming pods loaded underneath the wing of the aircraft. This type of testing was later repeated with EA1, the first Growler aircraft built, creating the same noise and vibration environment as aircraft E3.

In addition, VX-23's F/A-18E E10 BuNo 165537/SD100 was temporarily pulled from the Super Hornet test programme, fitted with instrumentation and used for a couple of weapon separation flights that each involved jettisoning an ALQ-99 pod.

E10 continues to serve with VX-23 for Super Hornet loads and jettison testing.

One of the reasons why the Growler developmental test programme proved so successful was because VX-23 had production standard Super Hornets and the flight clearances to assess most of the envelope. The squadron had completed a significant amount of the flutter, loads, flying qualities and performance testing before EA1 made its maiden flight from Boeing's production facility at St Louis-Lambert Field.

"That was the essence of why the four Super Hornets were configured as surrogate G-models to achieve that time advance," said Captain Jaime Engdahl, the then Growler programme lead with VX-23.

EA1 and EA2

On September 22, 2006, the first system design and development EA-18G Growler aircraft, EA1, arrived at Naval Air Station Patuxent River, Maryland, a month prior to its scheduled delivery date. It began its test programme with precision approach landing system flights before starting five months of mission systems testing in the anechoic chamber at Patuxent River. This involved assessment of on-board radar, receiver, and jammer compatibility, ALQ-218 emitter and characterisation testing, and ALQ-99 jammer testing.

The second development aircraft, EA2, arrived at Pax in late November.

EA1 and EA2 were both fitted with the advanced crew station, fully-functional ALQ-218 pods and fully-integrated ALQ-99 pods. EA1 was equipped with extensive analogue instrumentation (including that for ALQ-218, thermodynamic noise and vibration) and EA2 with equivalent digital systems.

Because of work already undertaken by VX-23 with the three G-representative Super Hornets, just under half of the aeromechanical flight test phase was complete before EA1 arrived at Pax River. The status of the aeromechanical phase at that time enabled the test team assigned to Air Test and Evaluation 23 (VX-23) to fly EA1 to an altitude of 35,000ft and up to 4.5g with a full mission load only days after its arrival at the Maryland base.

VX-23's Growler test programme's carrier suitability loading finished on October 27, 2006. It included catapult and arresting gear demonstrations with a mix of different Growler load configurations, some clean, some fully loaded and some asymmetric.

Bring Back

One aspect of carrier operations that differs between the Growler and the Super Hornet is the necessity for the EA-18G to bring back its full stores load to the ship. Bring back refers to the stores load an aircraft is permitted to land back on the carrier's flight deck, a design feature of all carrier-capable aircraft. Growlers only releasable stores (weapons) are AGM-88 HARM, AGM-88E AARGM and AIM-120 missiles.

As part of the suitability trials, VX-23 undertook a gross-weight expansion programme to increase the bring-back capability, including fuel – up from the Super Hornet's 44,000lb load to 48,000lb for the Growler.

An EA-18G aircraft was loaded to its heaviest configuration for catapult shots to ensure the tow-bar, nose-bar, gear and hook-point loads were within the required limits for launching the aircraft and arresting it with a gross weight of 48,000lb. Arrested landings were also conducted as part of the gross weight-expansion. This involved deceleration, high-sink landings, roll/yaw

In 2017, VAQ-142's CAG-bird was EA-18G BuNo 168381/NH500 seen at low-level, flying through a canyon in southern California. **Dan Stijovich**

landings and different attitudes simulated under various conditions.

The entire aeromechanical phase was completed in February 2007.

Flutter
Flutter testing was undertaken with F/A-18E Super Hornet 165779/SD101 for all stores to be carried by the EA-18G: the Growler stores-load configuration differs to the E and F-models.

In the spring of 2007, VX-23 was working through a 15-month mission systems flight test plan covering AIM-120 AMRAAM, AGM-88 HARM, Link-16, APG-79 radar, EDCM (Electronic Data Correlation Mechanism) and PALS (Precision Approach Landing System). EDCM is an algorithm that integrates all the electronic and link systems together.

Avionics Subsystem
The avionics subsystem combines the integration and automation needed for operability with the redundancy required to ensure flight safety and mission success. Key features of the system include integrated controls and displays, an inertial navigation set with carrier alignment capability, and extensive built-in test capability. The avionics subsystems operate under the control of two mission computers with primary data transfer between the mission computers and the other avionics equipment including the EAU via the mux buses and the high-speed data network.

US NAVY EA-18G GROWLER SQUADRONS

Electronic Attack Wing Pacific, Naval Air Station Whidbey Island, Washington

Squadron	Name	Carrier Air Wing	Tail code	Transition complete
VAQ-129	Vikings	FRS	NJ	2015
VAQ-130	Zappers	CVW-3	AC	January 2012
VAQ-133	Wizards	CVW-9	NG	June 2014
VAQ-136	Gauntlets	CVW-2	NE	March 2013
VAQ-137	Rooks	CVW-1	AB	October 2013
VAQ-139	Cougars	CVW-17	NA	October 2013
VAQ-140	Patriots	CVW-7	AG	July 2014
VAQ-142	Grey Wolves	CVW-11	NH	2015
VAQ-209	Star Warriors	TSW	AF	2014

Joint Expeditionary Squadrons, Naval Air Station Whidbey Island, Washington

Squadron	Name	Carrier Air Wing	Tail code	Transition complete
VAQ-131	Lancers		NL	2015
VAQ-132	Scorpions		NL	September 2009
VAQ-134	Garudas		NL	2016
VAQ-135	Black Ravens		NL	June 2011
VAQ-138	Yellowjackets		NL	August 2010
VAQ-144			NL	In work-up

Forward Deployed at Marine Corps Air Station Iwakuni, Japan

Squadron	Name	Carrier Air Wing	Tail code	Transition complete
VAQ-141	Shadowhawks	CVW-5	NF	February 2010

EA-18G GROWLER

An EA-18G Growler suspended inside NAVAIR's Air Combat Environment Test and Evaluation Facility at Patuxent River. Naval Air Systems Command for EMI testing. **Naval Air Systems Command**

Mission Computer System

The mission computer system consists of two digital computers (MC1 and MC2) which are high speed, stored program, programmable, general-purpose computers with core memory. Both MCs can provide the same basic navigation and weapon delivery back-up should the other MC fail.

The front and rear DDIs are driven directly by the MC over a high-speed interface bus, not by avionics mux bus commands. The HUD is driven directly by redundant connection to either MC. MC1 drives the front and rear left DDIs (see below) and HUD while MC2 drives the front and rear right DDIs and HUD.

Electronic Attack Unit (EAU)

The EAU provides the primary interface between the AEA subsystems and the AMC. Within the AEA suite, the EAU interfaces with the ALQ-218, ALQ-227 CCS, ALQ-99 pod suite and the MATT. The interface between the EAU and AMC consists of a High-Speed Data Network and MIL-STD-1553 bus interface. The EAU provides jammer management logic, manages AEA libraries, provides power control, and interfaces built-in-test for the AEA subsystems. The EAU coordinates aircraft navigation data with the AEA systems, provides EW track files for display and recording, and provides the audio interface between the AEA subsystems and the avionics suite.

Cockpit Controls and Displays

The cockpit controls and displays which are used for navigation operation are on the multipurpose display group.

The multipurpose display group consists of the right and left digital display indicators (DDIs), the multipurpose colour display (MPCD), the aft multipurpose colour display (AMPCD), the digital map set (DMS), the head-up display (HUD), the CRS (course) set switch, and the up-front control display (UFCD).

F/A-18F BuNo 165875/SD120 (F35) configured with Growler wing-tip pods and loaded with tow ALQ-99 test vehicles seen at Patuxent River in late 2004 ahead of a flying qualities mission. **Mark Ayton**

The multipurpose display group presents navigation, attack, and aircraft attitude displays to the pilot, and converts information received from the mission computer system to symbology for display on the DDIs, the MPCD, the UFCD, and the HUD. The HUD camera records the outside world and HUD symbology. The left and right DDIs, MPCD and the AMPCD contain pushbuttons for display selection and selection of various equipment operating modes. The UFCD is an active-matrix liquid crystal display with an infrared touchscreen for operator inputs.

Digital Display Indicators (DDIs)

The left and right DDI (LDDI/RDDI) are physically and functionally interchangeable, giving the ability to display desired information on either indicator. The left indicator is used primarily for stores status, built-in-test status, engine monitor, caution, and advisory displays. The right indicator is normally used for radar and weapon video displays. The DDIs have full colour capability in all display modes and are NVG compatible.

Multipurpose Colour Display (MPCD)

The MPCD is an NVG compatible digital display capable of providing any menu-selectable format except the video on the air-to-ground radar display. The MPCD drives itself using information received on the MUX.

Head-Up Display (HUD)

The HUD is on the centre main instrument panel and used as the primary flight instrument, weapon status, and weapon delivery display for the aircraft under all conditions. The HUD receives all symbology from MC1 or MC2, is electrically interfaced with the UFCD, and has NVG compatible raster display capability to allow it to display FLIR-fed video.

Up Front Control Display (UFCD)

The UFCD is on the main instrument panel below the HUD in the front cockpit. In the aft cockpit, the UFCD is located above the AMPCD. The UFCD is an active-matrix liquid crystal display with an infrared touchscreen used for data entry inputs, and control of the CNI systems - data link/radar beacon/ILS, autopilot modes, TACAN, IFF, UHF/VHF radios, radar altimeter, and AEA.

In addition, the touchscreen can be used as a multi-function display for display formats, including video. The UFCD is used in conjunction with the two DDIs, the AMPCD and the MPCD to enter navigation, sensor, electronic attack, and weapon delivery data. The UFCD is NVG compatible. The front and rear cockpit UFCDs operate independently.

Mission Systems Testing

Growlers EA1 and EA2 were the primary aircraft on which the mission systems performance was validated. In July 2007 the two aircraft were given the final build of software and shortly afterwards began the mission systems phase – comprising a 15-month flight test plan and programmes covering Link 16 data link, APG-79 AESA radar, ALQ-218 receiver, ALQ-99 tactical jamming system (including integration of its antenna patterns with the aircraft and electromagnetic compatibility), the ALQ-227 communication countermeasures system (including receiver performance and integration into the OFP jamming software), the interference cancellation system (including low-band testing and a complete survey of how well the system cancelled out jammer interference), AGM-88 HARM and AIM-120 AMRAAM missile integration including live firings, most of which was done at China Lake, and the electronic data correlation mechanism or EDCM, an algorithm that integrates all the electronic and link systems.

Testing of the data display and the electronic data correlation were key to Growler's mission success. Captain Engdahl explained: "With so much information being fed into the Growler's cockpit the concept behind EDCM was to fuse all data tracks and correlate electromagnetic information into single tracks that are useful to the crew.

"VX-23 spent considerable time operating over the Atlantic range making sure that EDCM was identifying specific emitters and correlating them in a useable form."

VX-23 also conducted RF (radio frequency) and a full electromagnetic compatibility programme for all the major systems like ALQ-99, ALQ-218, APG-79 and the MIDS data link to ensure each system could withstand the harsh electromagnetic environment (created by the wave forms of the radars, data links, antennas, and emitters) onboard a carrier and jamming in a combat environment.

The electromagnetic environment of a carrier is so severe that testing requires experts to sweep every conceivable RF waveform at the aircraft to ensure its integrity. During sea trials VX-23's test pilots did not encounter any RF compatibility issues.

Crew vehicle interface was another major programme in the mission systems phase and one that proved to be a big advantage to the aircraft. Captain Engdahl, who once served as an EA-6B Prowler ECMO values the level of integration afforded to Growler aircrew: "The data display and the EDCM and the fact that the ALQ-218, ALQ-227, ALQ-99 and the AESA radar all feed into a fused picture is what I like most about the aircraft. We had no problem going from a four-man crew [on the Prowler] to a two-man crew [on the Growler] because of the integrated capability."

The first release of live ordnance from an EA-18G Growler took place on July 23, 2008, which involved a successful shot of an AIM-120 AMRAAM missile against a BQM-74E target drone while jamming threat systems located at China Lake's Echo range. This was followed by a successful launch of an AGM-88 High-speed Anti-Radiation Missile (HARM) in early August.

VX-23 qualified the Growler for carrier operations during sea trials aboard the USS *Dwight D Eisenhower* (CVN-69) between July 31 and August 5, 2008. Owing to operational requirements of the *Eisenhower*, the squadron had just five days, half of the initial allotted time, to complete the tasks. VX-23 used Growler-configured Super Hornet E3 and the first production series EA-18G G1 to complete 319 approaches, 62 catapult shots and 62 arrested landings.

Captain Engdahl told the author that aircraft G1 was flawless in the carrier environment: "Its flying qualities were good, and the systems

Condensation swirls over the wings of an EA-18G assigned to Electronic Attack Squadron 130 (VAQ-130) 'Zappers' after the pilot flew by the aircraft carrier USS *Dwight D Eisenhower* (CVN 69) during its 2016 deployment. **US Navy/VAQ-130**

This image shot from the cockpit of an EA-18G shows the wing fold midway through its fold-up cycle on board the aircraft carrier USS *Theodore Roosevelt* (CVN 71). **US Navy/VAQ-142**

In July 2004, NAVAIR dedicated three Super Hornet aircraft to the Growler flight test programme which included F/A-18E BuNo 165167/SD101 (E3). The aircraft, used for carrier suitability and flight loads, is seen hot-pit refuelling at Patuxent River in late 2004 when configured with Growler wing-tip pods. **Mark Ayton**

EA-18G GROWLER

On September 22, 2006, the first System Design and Development EA-18G Growler aircraft, EA1, arrived at Naval Air Station Patuxent River, Maryland, a month prior to its scheduled delivery date. **Naval Air Systems Command**

GROWLER CAPABILITY MODIFICATION

On March 19, 2021, PMA-265 commenced the five-year Growler Capability Modification (GCM) programme at Naval Air Station Whidbey Island, Washington - the first major upgrade of the EA-18G Growler's capabilities in a new aircraft modification line at the sprawling base.

The March 19 inductee was rolled-out after GCM during the final week of July which subsequently entered its flight test programme and a second GCM-configured aircraft followed during at the end of August.

Captain Steve May, PMA-265's deputy programme manager for EA-18G Growler said GCM is a mid-tier enhancement to the platform that combines a number of improvements to the airframe, replacement of some outdated boxes, wiring enhancements to the new NGJ-MB pylon, and multiple engineering change proposals (modifications) of several EA-18G aircraft sub-systems.

GCM includes enhancements to the airborne electronic attack system and the ALQ-218 receiver system designed to enable operation in complex electromagnetic environments, and integration of an advanced datalink and the ALQ-249(V)1 NGJ-MB pod itself.

According to Cpt May, many of the enhancements destined for the aircraft and the cockpits that will support integration of the NGJ-MB and its expanded functionality is facilitated by the current H16 and subsequent H18 OFPs.

performed well. The only thing that surprised us was a sluggish wave-off." This refers to the amount of time [a couple of seconds] that's required for the aircraft's engines to spool-up and fly away [climb] when the landing signals officer waves-off the landing. A Growler requires a little more time to wave-off and go around especially when landing with a 48,000lb maximum trap weight.

At the conclusion of the developmental flight-test programme in October 2008, VX-23 had undertaken 346 sorties including 991 flight hours for mission systems testing.

EA-18G Hardware

The Growler's primary antennas and sensors are housed in two ALQ-218 wing-tip pods. Additional antennas located on the forward and aft of the aircraft provide the separation required for the ALQ-218 system to correctly process signals.

The EA-18G is not armed with a cannon, its gun-bay or nose pallet houses much of the ALQ-218 system, the ALQ-227 Communications Countermeasures System (CCS) and Electronic Attack Unit (EAU) avionics. On a Super Hornet the space houses a hydraulically driven, six-barrelled, air-cooled, electrically fired 20mm M61 cannon.

The ALQ-218 digital receiver system can detect threats throughout the RF spectrum by measuring in small elements. When the ALQ-218 intercepts a signal (detects a target) the target is handed over to a secondary receiver. The secondary receiver takes very fine and parametric measurements of a signal's frequency and amplitude. The system calculates the position of a ground-based threat emitter by measuring differences in phase (or waveform angle) relative to the aircraft's position in time, a method known as interferometry.

A CCS antenna is carried on the top of the fuselage. EA1 and EA2 were retrofitted with CCS in the spring of 2007.

Growler inherited the Multi-purpose Advanced Tactical Terminal (MATT) satellite communications receiver originally used by the EA-6B. MATT is fixed on the aft top of the fuselage providing a satellite link to the aircraft.

ALQ-99 pods fitted to the Growler have modified backs and radomes to help with higher g-loads. Low-band antennas are housed in a profiled radome (profiled in cross section) while those used for high-band antennas are straight.

The EA-18G has a new interference cancellation system, known as INCANS, designed to enable UHF communication to be made during jamming.

Cockpit

Growler system software is embedded into the standard H-series release used on F/A-18E and F/A-18F Super Hornets using the same cockpit hardware for the electronic attack role. A standard F-model loaded with H-series software has two levels of display. The Growler has a third level showing all the electronic attack options, which

is only activated by recognition of the aircraft's electronic attack systems and the ALQ-218. Hands on throttle and stick (HOTAS) control allows aircrew to view, operate from and switch between all three levels of display. The four primary displays in the aft cockpit are inter-linked, including to the front seat allowing the pilot and WSO to operate with full crew co-ordination.

Operational Evaluation
Air Test and Evaluation Squadron 9 (VX-9) 'Vampires', based at Naval Air Weapons Station China Lake, commenced the Growler's four-month Operational Evaluation (OPEVAL) in November 2008 using the first three production aircraft, G1, G2 and G3. All three aircraft were

F/A-18F BuNo 165875/SD120 assigned to Air Test and Evaluation Squadron 23 (VX-23) was used to fly NGJ-MB test vehicles for flight tests in October 2020. **US Navy/Steve Wolff**

Below left to right: Simultaneous catapult launches from the aircraft carrier USS *Dwight D Eisenhower* (CVN 69), an EA-18G in the lead and an F/A-18E Super Hornet to the right. **US Navy/VAQ-130**

An EA-18G launches from the number four waist catapult on board the USS *Nimitz* (CVN 68) during its 2021 deployment. Note how the aircraft's left side ALQ-218 wing tip pod is over the side edge of the flight deck. **US Navy/CVN 68/VAQ-139**

initially delivered to Pax River and used for various test programmes. During the final nine months of developmental testing, aircrews from VX-9 were flown in G2 and G3 to gain familiarity with the Growler's complex systems. All three aircraft were delivered to China Lake in August 2008 to be used by VX-9 for a further three months of aircrew and maintenance training before OPEVAL commenced. VX-9 conducted integrated operational test and evaluation at China Lake between October 1, 2008, and May 4, 2009, and included 471 flight test hours.

On July 29, 2009, the Department of Defense released the findings of the OPEVAL: the aircraft received the rating of operationally effective, operationally suitable and was recommended for fleet introduction.

The US Navy's application of integrated testing of the EA-18G enabled early identification of areas of risk which provided more time to aggressively pursue resolution of risk areas and deficiencies.

During IOT&E the EA-18G participated in multiple operational test events, including large force exercises at Nellis Air Force Base, Nevada in December 2008 which provided an operational environment to better assess interoperability with the US Air Force and other agencies. This included use of the Multi-functional Information Distribution System and Link-16 to pass information on targeting and threat radar site locations to other aircraft tasked with attacking targets on the Nevada Test and Training Range as part of large strike packages operating from Nellis and other locations.

Naval Air Systems Command also conducted operational testing on China Lake's electronic combat range dubbed the echo range, a facility laced with some of the most capable threat emitters and associated range instrumentation used for electronic warfare threat environment simulation. NAVAIR's test squadrons also deployed on board the USS *John C Stennis* (CVN 74) for carrier suitability testing.

At the time of the director, operational test, and evaluation's FY2009 Annual Report, the EA-18G was deemed operationally effective, but not operationally suitable based upon poor maintainability associated with ALQ-218 BIT performance and interface with the legacy ALQ-99 jamming pods. NAVAIR duly conducted what's known as a verification of correction of deficiencies (VCD) testing between September 2009 and January 2010. Testing primarily assessed software improvements which are designed to resolve maintainability shortfalls in ALQ-218 built-in-test (BIT) performance and its interface with the legacy ALQ-99 jamming pods. All test objectives were completed during 150 flight hours and over 90 sorties from multiple sites including Nellis Air Force Base.

The VCD test results provided robust evidence that aircraft software stability was improving, particularly related to BIT maturation, but additional development and flight testing was required to confirm the problems had been resolved.

In May 2010, the DOT&E released a VCD test report memorandum to NAVAIR that assessed the performance of the suitability improvements and provided NAVAIR with recommendations for FOT&E in the early part of FY2011.

EA-18G FOT&E was subsequently conducted between November 2010 and June 2011 to assess the latest SCS H6E software load and fixes for the maintainability problems. The FOT&E test programme involved 115.2 flight hours over 70 test sorties. Test efforts included evaluation of the Civilian Instrument Landing System integration into the EA-18G, a capability designed to enhance safe operations from civilian airfields as part of expeditionary (non-aircraft carrier) situations.

FOT&E test results demonstrated that the EA-18G remained operationally effective, with results that met most of the thresholds deemed necessary for operational availability requirements. Maintainability did not meet the threshold level but only by a small measure, and built-in test performance was largely improved since the IOT&E. Maintenance documentation had improved from IOT&E, but US Navy personnel still rated the system as difficult to use and incomplete in some areas. DOT&E's complete assessment was published in Q1 FY2012, which deemed the EA-18G weapon system as operationally effective and operationally suitable.

Fleet Introduction

Naval Air Station Whidbey Island in Washington state is the Growler master jet base and home to Electronic Attack Squadron 129 (VAQ-129) 'Vikings', the Growler Fleet Replacement Squadron. Under the original transition schedule, the first US Navy aircrew commenced training on a F-model with Boeing at St Louis in 2007.

The first EA-18G production aircraft G4 was accepted by VAQ-129 at Whidbey on June 3, 2008. Today, 14 fleet squadrons are based at Whidbey with the 15th forward deployed to Marine Corps Air Station Iwakuni, Japan. Six of the 14 squadrons based at Whidbey are expeditionary VAQ squadrons which support US Air Force and US Navy shore-based operations.

Each Electronic Attack squadron has six EA-18Gs assigned.

Growler initial operating capability was achieved in Q4 FY2009, when VAQ-129 and the first frontline squadron were fully established with four and five aircraft, respectively.

Expeditionary squadron, VAQ-132 'Scorpions' undertook the first shore-based combat deployment between October 2010 and July 2011, followed by VAQ-141 'Shadowhawks' which set sail onboard the USS *George H W Bush* (CVN 77) in May 2011 for the Growler's inaugural carrier deployment.

Initial training and maintenance support was undertaken at Naval Air Station Lemoore, California. The first cadre of aircrew received familiarisation training on the F-model with VFA-122 at Lemoore, and those crews moved to Whidbey for the arrival of the first production aircraft.

Manned-Unmanned: Demonstrating Control Using Artificial Intelligence

According to the Navy Warfare Development Command, the US Navy's Fleet Experimentation (FLEX) programme examines various solutions to capability gaps identified by Warfighting Development Centers and Navy Urgent Operational Needs Statements. Additionally, the FLEX programme addresses innovative concepts, tactics, techniques, and procedures, and concepts of operation that collectively mitigate Fleet-identified capability gaps.

Experimentation activities include live events and campaigns designed to evaluate tangible materiel and non-materiel solutions to enhance the fleet's ability to conduct assigned missions. Design, planning, systems engineering, integration, execution, data collection, analysis and assessment are included in support of campaigns and live events.

FLEX is a programme that supports elements of the Secretary of the Navy's innovation vision and includes acceleration of emerging operational capabilities for strike and expeditionary warfare, and information dominance, to the Fleet.

The FLEX staged in October 2019 included three EA-18G Growler electronic attack aircraft operating from Naval Air Station Patuxent River, Maryland, home of Naval Air Systems Command and the Naval Air Warfare Center Aircraft Division. Assigned to Air Test and Evaluation Squadron 23 (VX-23), the three Growlers were fitted with a control system called Artificial Reasoning and Cognition (ARC) and prototypes of the Distributed Targeting Processor-Networked (DTP-N) and Tactical Targeting Network Technology (TTNT).

The name of the control system implies it's an artificial intelligence (AI) machine (computer) that mimics the reasoning and cognitive functions of the human mind, specifically learning and problem solving, respectively. Within AI a machine learning system identifies patterns within data sets and thus tries to make predictions based on the existing data, and a machine reasoning system solves problems in an ambiguous and

Sailors load ordnance onto an EA-18G Growler assigned to Electronic Attack Squadron 136 (VAQ-136) 'Gauntlets' on the flight deck of the aircraft carrier USS *Carl Vinson* (CVN 70). The Gauntlets were participating in an exercise that involved simulated strikes on naval targets off the coast of Okinawa, Japan. **US Navy/Mass Communication Specialist 2nd Class Jonteil Johnson**

Sailors assigned to Electronic Attack Squadron 135 (VAQ-135) 'Black Ravens' prepare an EA-18G Growler for flight during snowy conditions at Naval Air Facility Misawa, Japan. **US Navy/Mass Communication Specialist 2nd Class Jan David De Luna Mercado**

EA-18G GROWLER

changing environment using available knowledge and logical techniques like deduction and induction. Both machines have direct application in the control of autonomous systems.

The DTP-N functions like a big computer to improve the aircraft's computer processing power, while the TTNT is a high-capacity data pipe that increases the amount of data flow on and off the aircraft. Combined, the two systems make the aircraft a smart node on networks, known by the clunky name, Naval Integrated Fire Control-Counter Air.

The three systems enabled two of the Growler aircraft to be operated as unmanned autonomously controlled surrogate aircraft, and the third as a control station: a concept known as manned-unmanned teaming or MUMT. Each surrogate aircraft had a safety pilot on board who performed the take-off and landing.

Jointly funded by Naval Air Systems Command and Boeing, the demonstration help validate technology that enables an EA-18G Growler to fly autonomously as an unmanned electronic attack air system with the ability to operate some of its sensors; in this case the APG-79 active electronically scanned array radar. According to the official release, the surrogate fighters were flown in multiple pre-set formations and linked air-to-air sensor [captured by the radar] data via the TTNT to the manned aircraft.

Given the complex electronic attack and jamming mission performed by the system-laden Growler, this proof-of-concept experiment is likely to be the first step toward further flight trials in which jamming pods and mission systems are operated autonomously.

This likely objective was not mentioned in Boeing's official release, but the company claims the technology used in the demonstration enables the Navy to extend the reach of sensors while keeping manned aircraft out of harm's way. Well, in this experiment the sensors were on the surrogate aircraft and the manned aircraft was likely to have been positioned at a stand-off range and therefore out of harm's way.

Boeing has not confirmed if the ARC system is a propriety company product or how long the system has been in development but did confirm the ARC control system used in FLEX 2019 is a separate effort from the Boeing Defence Australia's Airpower Teaming Systems, the so-called loyal wingman concept of ops. Boeing told the author that though the two projects *may* have similar goals regarding manned-unmanned teaming, they are separate efforts.

Software used by the ARC, DTP-N and the aircraft's mission computer were all specifically developed for the FLEX demonstrations but based on Growler's current H14 Operational Flight Program.

Despite Boeing's official release stating it [the ARC] could provide synergy with other Navy unmanned systems in development across the [warfare] spectrum, the company would not confirm if the ARC were a derivation of the control system used by Boeing's MQ-25 Stingray unmanned Carrier-Based Aerial-Refuelling System.

Hardware modifications comprised radios and associated antennas for the TTNT system.

Over the course of four flights, each involving the three modified Growler aircraft, 21 demonstrations were completed, Boeing would not provide any specific examples.

Appropriately, Boeing describes the concept as a force multiplier that enables a single aircrew to control multiple aircraft without greatly increasing workload. The term 'multiple aircraft' meaning both unmanned aircraft and unmanned air vehicles such as the Growler and MQ-25 Stingray, respectively.

Naval Air Systems Command told the author that data from the demonstration is being analysed for future consideration. It seems likely that further application of the concept will be forthcoming to ensure the Growler weapon system continues to protect all strike aircraft during high-threat missions.

An EA-18G Growler assigned to Electronic Attack Squadron 141 (VAQ-141) 'Shadowhawks' launches from the flight deck of the aircraft carrier USS *Ronald Reagan* (CVN 76) during Exercise Keen Sword 21. **US Navy/Mass Communication Specialist 3rd Class Gabriel Martinez**

Growler's Continuous Improvement

As part of the Growler's road map, the aircraft is continually improved primarily by the roughly biennial introduction of new operational flight program software drops. As a backdrop to the latest H14 software, the previous H12 release included another phase of multi-sensor integration improvements, enhanced ALQ-218 geolocation, communication countermeasures set improvements, display improvements (symbology and crew-vehicle interface) to enhance air-to-surface, air-to-air and counter electronic attack sensor integration to manage aircrew workload, and additional capabilities to operate in ATC-controlled airspace.

The latest, H14, commenced operational test in October 2018, concluded earlier this year, and has just been released to the fleet to meet the latest operational requirements. Last March, Naval Air Systems Command staged numerous fire control missions in an electronic attack environment at the sea test range off the coast of California.

In July, live fire missile testing was undertaken to demonstrate the integration of the AIM-120 AMRAAM missile with the Super Hornet and Growler aircraft operating with the H14 software.

PMA-265 is now underway with the developmental test of the subsequent H16 software which will provide:
- Software and hardware upgrades to the ALQ-218 digital receiver.
- An open architecture, multi-level secure processor known as the Distributed Tactical Processor-Network (DTP-N) said to be 17-times more powerful than the original Growler system.
- The Tactical Targeting Networking Technology (TTNT), a high throughput, low latency datalink called with satellite communications for advanced network connectivity.

Equipped with DTP-N and TTNT, a pair of Growlers will be able to fuse data acquired by on board and off board sensors to generate a common tactical picture of the battlespace and rapidly exchange that information with other assets. What does that achieve? It enhances targeting capabilities and improves air-to-air timelines and performance. This capability is scheduled to be implemented with several H-series software builds.

Back in August 2017, the Navy staged a series of fleet experiments called Netted Sensors 2017 conducted by the Navy Warfare Development Command involving, amongst others, F/A-18 Super Hornet and EA-18G Growler aircraft.

Focus of the experiments was sensor networking over the TTNT data link to enable distribution of information from around the maritime battlespace to all participating assets, aircraft, ships, and shore stations.

EA-18Gs were focused on working a common tactical picture, multi-ship electronic surveillance, Growler manned-unmanned teaming, and network-centric collaborative targeting (NCCT) technologies. Which put simply means using joint data standards and interfaces to speed up sensor cueing and targeting through to launching strikes in multi-sensor geolocation events.

Cpt Denney outlined other initiatives to deliver new capability to the fleet faster to outpace potential threats, to improve and sustain aircraft mission capability rates by using predictive maintenance to spend time performing effective and proactive maintenance rather than reactive maintenance.

One change already in effect and in support of the above is migration from multi-sensor integration to multi-system integration. This allows for insertion of innovative technologies and requirements to keep pace with the fleet's demands; this will continue with H16.

BLOCK II GROWLER

Ongoing work is defining the Block II Growler's capability development programme. Included are the advanced crew station featuring a large area display and low-profile head-up display which will initially deploy on the Block III Super Hornet and then migrate to the Block II Growler, with installations potentially beginning in FY2025.

Growlers are not equipped with a cannon, but the internal space is not left empty, it's fitted out with an airborne electronic attack palette; this will be replaced on the Block II configuration to overcome obsolescence.

Given the small fleet of aircraft, their ongoing utilisation rates, and an out-of-service date currently pitched for the mid-2040s, PMA-265 is already conducting a service life assessment programme to assess utilisation and when a service life extension programme will need to start. Captain Denney explained that because of the Growler's utilisation, a service life extension programme will not start until after conversion to the Block II is complete and forecast 2025 as the year for the Block II Growler's initial operational capability declaration.

When asked whether the PMA-265 team will be able to stay ahead of fast developing emerging threats, Denney said it was the team's number one mission. He said: "Our motto is to support, to sustain and advance the fleet to ensure the aircraft is able to fight and win against potential adversaries, which is why we make incremental improvements. We are developing the Block II Growler to exceed the capabilities of our potential adversaries."

EA-18G GROWLER

This image: F/A-18F BuNo 165875/SD120 in EA-18G configuration on a flying qualities mission from Patuxent River on October 21, 2020, fitted with a nose boom and two ALQ-249 test vehicles. **US Navy/Steve Wolff**

Right: A computer-generated image of an early NGJ design, which is different to the ALQ-249 now undergoing flight test. **Raytheon**

TACTICAL JAMMING SYSTEMS

Mark Ayton provides an overview of the EA-18G Growler's ALQ-99 and ALQ-249 tactical jamming systems.

THE EA-18G AIRCRAFT is only part of the Growler weapons system. The electronic attack mission is conducted by the ALQ-99 tactical jamming system which has been in US Navy operation since 1971. Continual upgrades have enabled the ALQ-99 to remain relevant against potential threats from around the world. Distinct types of ALQ-99 pod are dedicated to notional wave bands and therefore target sets and what the attack solution should be. Over the past 35 years, the ALQ-99 has been upgraded in diverse ways; by either wave band, by radio frequency exciter or by universal exciter. Back in 2005 the ALQ-99 system hit its technology ceiling. Certain new target sets can be accommodated with small tweaks to the system, those of a communication or asymmetric warfare type, but for the latest surface-to-air missile systems, the ceiling was inhibitive. New architecture was required. An alternative of alternatives for a Next Generation Jammer (NGJ) was undertaken and completed in April 2010. That November, a resources, requirements, and review (R3) board sat at the Pentagon, which provided validation to build the system for use by the EA-18G.

Providing sufficient power and cooling for an electronic attack capability on a tactical size aircraft is a big challenge. There's a trade-off between power and range which is constrained by physics: the more power the more generation required, but the EA-18G does not generate a lot of excess power so power generation needs to be built into the pod. The ALQ-99 uses externally-mounted RAM air turbines, a pitched propeller that generates a lot of power. That's not an option for the NGJ because the amount of electrical power needed to meet the ALQ-249's effective isotropic radiated power (output power) requirements drove the need for an internal RAM air turbine generator dubbed the RAT G. The ALQ-99's externally-mounted RAT does not generate enough power to meet the ALQ-249's required output power.

Arrays also present unique challenges. An active electronically scanned array radar works best using a large flat plate, an arrangement that allows a good beam to be formed by focussing a lot of energy. Electronic attack is no different but for the

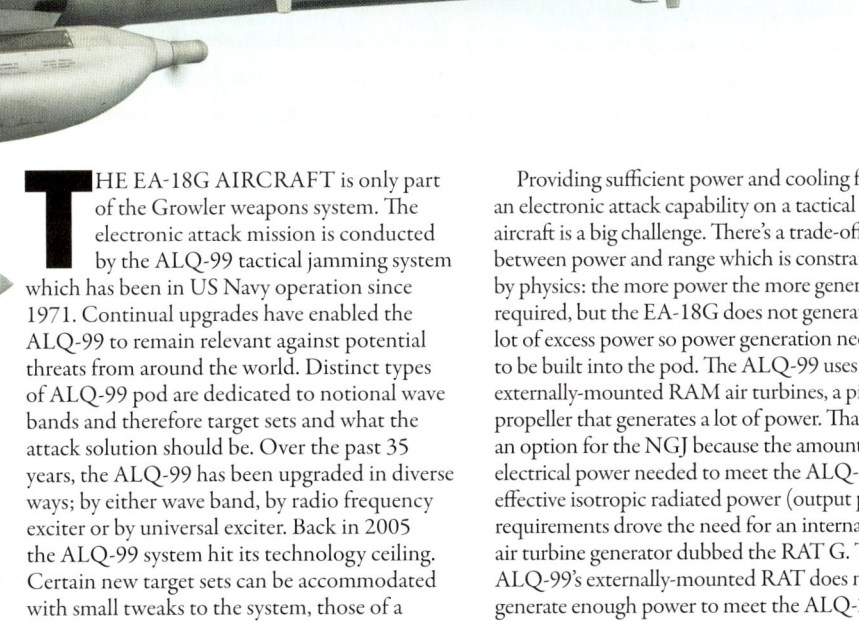

requirement to have almost a 100% duty cycle active array for full-on jamming, and this requires efficient beam formers and amplifiers.

NGJ uses Gallium Nitride-based devices. Gallium Nitride based electronic technology was one of the necessary technologies that needed to be matured to enable the required close to 100% duty cycle jamming capability. A single follow-on technology development contract was awarded to Raytheon in July 2013.

Next Generation Jammer

Under the Joint Electronics Type Designation System, the NGJ Mid-band is dubbed the ALQ-249; a high-powered, agile, electronic attack system capable of operating at stand-off ranges, attacking multiple targets simultaneously with advanced jamming techniques designed for rapid upgrades with a modular, open systems architecture.

Equipped with agile, active electronically scanned arrays and an all-digital back end, the ALQ-249 conducts precise jamming assignments against advanced and emerging threats operating throughout a wide range of radio frequency bands.

Confronted with integrated air defence system radars, communications, and data links, the ALQ-249's ability to engage threat systems and conduct robust jamming at standoff distances is vital. Consequently, the ALQ-249 must provide sufficient effective isotropic radiated power (EIRP) - the measured radiated (output) power of an antenna in a specific direction.

EA-18G GROWLER

NGJ-MB is built with open, modular architecture, which can accommodate rapid upgrades. **Raytheon**

NGJ-MB pods on the production line at Raytheon Technologies' facilities in Forest, Mississippi. **Raytheon**

NGJ-MB pods on the production line at Raytheon Technologies' facilities in Forest, Mississippi. The NGJ-MB can be scaled for different missions and aircraft types. **Raytheon**

In addition to the technical complexity and the necessary size and all-up weight restrictions of a new-generation electronic attack pod, the NGJ design team was faced with other constraints. Its parent aircraft, the EA-18G Growler, is a carrier capable tactical aircraft which endures the rigour of flight deck catapult launches and arrested landings - a very demanding environment. Its operation involves emission of electromagnetic and directed energy to degrade, neutralise or destroy an enemy's combat capability, which requires careful control and management to ensure both the aircrew and the aircraft are not adversely affected.

So, what are the defining design drivers for the NGJ pod? According to Captain Orr there are four.

- Power requirement, driven by operational scenarios.
- Power generation capability, which defines the cooling requirement.
- Processing power, which must enable all the pod's combat functions, many of which are automated.
- And airworthiness, which includes integration constraints, structural limits, and system software integration.

In performance terms, each of the four elements had to be balanced and optimised against each other to produce the required capability.

Once integrated on the EA-18G, the ALQ-249 will be capable of contributing to the full range of warfare from air strikes in anti-access/area denial environments to the type of irregular warfare encountered in Afghanistan.

The ALQ-249 pod is approximately 14ft (4.27m) long with a fuselage diameter close to 30in (760mm).

One outcome of the November 2010 R3 board was to return the NGJ programme into incremental capabilities.

- Increment 1 will be used to deny, degrade, or deceive use of the electromagnetic spectrum employing both reactive and pre-emptive jamming techniques and is currently in the Engineering and Manufacturing Development (EMD) phase.
- Increment 2 is the low-band (now known as NGJ Low Band), which brings capability to the lower frequencies of the electromagnetic spectrum and includes capability against additional target sets, with IOC targeted for 2025. This effort plans to formally commence in FY2020.
- Increment 3 (now known as NGJ High Band) will bring capability to the higher frequencies of the electromagnetic spectrum.

A typical Block 1 EA-18G load-out comprises three ALQ-99 pods, two AGM-88 HARMs or two AGM-88E AARGMs, two AIM-120 AMRAAMs and two drop tanks, with a launch weight of 66,000lb.

April 2016 was an important month for the NGJ Mid-Band programme - it received Milestone B approval to enter EMD, and Raytheon was awarded a 56-month contract valued at US$1bn for execution of the EMD phase. In accordance with the contract, Raytheon will deliver 15 engineering development model pods to be used for mission systems testing and qualification, and 14 aeromechanical pods for airworthiness certification.

On April 27, 2017, the NGJ programme completed its critical design review which identified deficiencies that deemed a redesign of the pod structure, which caused schedule and cost breaches to the programme. Despite the structure redesign development, manufacturing, integration and testing of the antenna arrays, power generation system, software, common electronics unit continued, in accordance with the EA-18G H16 software integration schedule.

On October 18, 2017, a memorandum of understanding was signed with Australia forming a joint program office and a cooperative development programme. The Royal Australian Air Force is the only other air arm currently operating the EA-18G Growler.

Testing

In early 2020, Naval Air System Command's anechoic chamber at Patuxent River was occupied by an EA-18G Growler aircraft fitted with the first set of two engineering development model mission system pods.

The aircraft and pods were first placed in the chamber in November 2019, and to date have undertaken over 400 hours of testing with both pods radiating to check basic pod functionality and to capture electromagnetic interference data. The latter being the measurement of radiation data which is used to ensure the pod does not overheat or adversely affect the aircraft and the aircrew. Data captured in the chamber is also being used to gain an interim flight clearance authorisation to operate a Growler aircraft fitted with a set of NGJ pods in non-standard configurations, flight envelopes, or conditions.

An NGJ-MB pod on the production line. The first NGJ-MB pod was delivered to Naval Air Systems Command in July 2019. Raytheon

EA-18G GROWLER

The chamber testing is now providing real data, as opposed to analysed data, for use in the mission system modelling process to begin validation of the system. Prior to that, extensive mission system modelling of the pod's application to electronic attack and jamming was based entirely on analysed data captured from ALQ-99 pods in operational scenarios.

Stores Integration

In the summer of 2019, Raytheon delivered the first NGJ Mid-Band EMD pod to Patuxent River to begin initial stores integration. This included verification of ground procedures, mass properties, aircraft installation, and built-in test checks, all in preparation for chamber and flight testing.

Diverse types of tests require different configurations of pods such as fatigue, static, jettison and aeromechanical versions; the latter used for flying qualities and aircraft integration. Pods used for mission system testing are in full-up configuration with all the sub-systems installed. Unsurprisingly, mission system pods are expensive and are unnecessary for some elements of the flight test programme.

Prior to first flight, the NGJ pod is undergoing all the standard tests required for stores integration. Static strength testing was completed in the early autumn of 2019. Once flights began, a set of NGJ pods underwent captive carriage tests: loads, environmental, flying qualities, performance, drag and structural integrity. Performance and jettison tests will follow as part of the employment phase.

Captain Orr described the NGJ flight test programme as thorough and extensive, involving hundreds of missions. It will involve aero mechanical testing of the pod's physical integration on the aircraft; mission systems testing of the pod's performance, and carrier suitability testing.

Air Test and Evaluation Squadron 23 (VX-23) will conduct the NGJ flight test programme. The squadron hosts five Growler aircraft and will receive a series of pods during March and April for the flight test programme; the set of pods currently in the chamber will not be used for flight tests.

Chamber testing will continue for quite some time as its focus changes to increased performance. Milestone C, the low-rate initial production decision, is anticipated at the end of FY2020. Flight testing began in the spring and continued through most of 2021.

An operational test readiness review should take place by early 2022. If the review is successful, the NGJ pod will enter operational test that year, followed by an initial operating capability declaration in FY2022.

Gulfstream III Flight Testing

Last year, Raytheon contracted Calspan to fly its Gulfstream III test bed aircraft fitted with a test pod designed specifically for power generation testing and risk reduction efforts in support of the NGJ's initial flight clearance process.

Raytheon's NGJ test pod was configured with a RAT G to demonstrate the functionality, mechanical interfaces, and controls of the RAM air turbine.

The turbine's design requirements are significant to such an extent the Gulfstream test flights were planned from the start of the programme and named the prime power generation capability or PPGC.

Captain Orr said the flight test was conducted as a risk reduction effort because the RAT G was identified as having risk early in the NGJ programme. NAVAIR set the test objectives and observed the flights conducted by Raytheon and Calspan. Explaining, he said: "There really were

Two NGJ-MB pods fitted with all functioning mission systems installed, loaded on the underwing inner pylons of EA-18G BuNo 166641/SD521. This was the second flight of mission system pods on September 3, 2021. **Naval Air Systems Command**

no surprises during the test flights. The objective was to validate some of the assumptions we held, but the data captured did not lead to any design changes."

Operational Flight Programs
Not surprisingly, the NGJ pod runs on its own operational flight programme (OFP) software, which is independent, but entirely aligned with the Growler aircraft's own OFP. The Growler runs on high order language OFPs designated by the letter H. The NGJ will be integrated and enter fleet service with EA-18G Growler aircraft using H16 software. So critical is alignment of the two OFPs that the PMA-234 NGJ programme office has an NGJ integration team that works daily with the PMA-265 Growler programme office team. Captain Orr said PMA-234 staff understand the H16 software schedule and the releases and tie the NGJ pod releases, from a capability perspective to the corresponding H16 releases to ensure that when H16 is delivered to the fleet it will be able to use NGJ.

Explaining the process, Cpt Orr said: "We use the interface control documents issued to us by PMA-265, for hardware and software, and fully understand what the constraints are with H16. If we need to update the pod's software, to the maximum extent possible we design it such that we can update the pod without having to touch the H16 OFP. If a situation arose in which we wanted to add capability to the pod that would not run on the existing aircraft OFP, we would likely delay until the next aircraft OFP was released.

Given that electronic warfare is a constantly evolving tit-for-tat capability, an electronic attack pod needs to keep a pace with emerging threats. This requires Naval electronic warfare labs to be able to quickly tweak the pod's capability without the need to change the pod's OFP. According to Orr the pod's capability can be updated for most conditions independent of the OFP.

Chamber Testing
Preliminary NGJ-MB chamber testing began in November 2019 and continued until summer 2020, taking place mostly at NAVAIR's Air Combat Environment Test and Evaluation Facility (ACETEF) and its High-power Electronic Attack Technique Radiation (HEATR) Chamber.

The aircraft and pods undertook hundreds of hours of testing with both pods radiating to check basic pod functionality and to capture electromagnetic interference data. The latter being the measurement of radiation data which is used to ensure the pod does not overheat or adversely affect the aircraft and the aircrew. Data captured in the chamber was also used to gain an interim flight clearance authorisation to operate a Growler aircraft fitted with a set of NGJ pods in non-standard configurations, flight envelopes, or conditions.

The chamber testing provided real data, as opposed to analysed data, for use in the mission system modelling process to begin validation of the system.

NAVAIR then began executing trial developmental runs for NGJ-MB in the ACETEF along with its jammer technique generation testing in the HEATR chamber, in August 2020. Developmental design of experiment runs for score were scheduled to begin in November 2020. NAVAIR plans to complete a representative set of jammer technique test points in the HEATR lab to support Milestone C, as well as preliminary EIRP testing in the ACETEF chamber.

In addition to the significant effort required to integrate the NGJ-MB pods to operate in the facilities, other tests completed include hazard of electromagnetic radiation to personnel, along with pod functionality and performance tests. Functionality demonstrated includes making jammer assignments with full, half, and quarter arrays; timing and beam commutation between assignments; and radiation from two full arrays.

Flight Testing

Pax River-based VX-23 is using two types of NGJ-MB pods for the test programme: instrumented aeromechanical pods or AMPs, and mission system pods capable of radiating.

The squadron loaded an instrumented aeromechanical pod on an EA-18G for the first time in October 2020, for aeromechanical flight test.

VX-23 started the flying qualities portion between October and December in powered approach configuration flying with the landing gear and flaps down, first evaluating take-off and landing.

Between May and August 2021, VX-23 started the envelope expansion programme to determine the effects the pod has on the aircraft's overall performance, beginning with powered approach configuration.

At the time of writing, the envelope expansion programme was on pause so the aircraft could be engineered ahead of starting opposite way configuration performance testing with the landing gear and flaps retracted.

Before the end of the year, VX-23 expects to start the jettison portion using a mass model property test article, a copy of an NGJ-MB pod without the functional arrays and computers, designed for mass model properties determination during separation from the aircraft.

One of the biggest test events yet to come, which has considerable bearing on the programme, is that of doors-open performance testing.

A pod has articulating doors at its mid-fuselage position which are opened during flight to provide air flow cooling to the power generation systems within.

An NGJ pod changes shape when its doors open and close. Determining how the doors change in terms of aeromechanics, aircraft handling and loads is essential. Consequently, the flight-test programme will include an in-depth aeromechanical portion to ensure loads on the aircraft and the pod are acceptable throughout the flight envelope.

The NGJ-MB flight test programme will be the first time an F/A-18 series aircraft has ever carried a pod that changes its shape during flight. This one aspect raises a million-dollar question for the US Navy, how will the aircraft fly with a large, heavy, shape-changing pod on each wing?

The performance testing sequence starts with the doors-closed to characterise the configuration, then doors-closed in the opposite way configuration, followed by doors-open in both powered approach and opposite way configuration. To date all flights have involved doors-closed performance testing.

The Growler has an inherent flight envelope limit which the aircraft will be flown up to in all the flight test disciplines such as performance, flying qualities, aeroelastic, and loads.

When VX-23 flew an NGJ on a Growler for the first time in August 2020, the pod involved was a mission system version. It proved to be a build-up flight, followed by a second successful mission which involved the first radiation with the pod and the aircraft successfully communicating. During September, VX-23 accomplished the first radiation with a full-up mission systems NGJ-MB pod.

To expedite the programme, PMA-234 and VX-23 are concurrently undertaking mission systems and aeromechanical testing, an unusual arrangement, since the aeromechanical portion usually builds up an envelope ahead of mission systems testing.

Consequently, each time the envelope is increased, the mission systems can be cleared out to higher speeds and loads, which reduces the timeline.

Below: A computer-generated image of an early configuration of the ALQ-249 pod. Raytheon

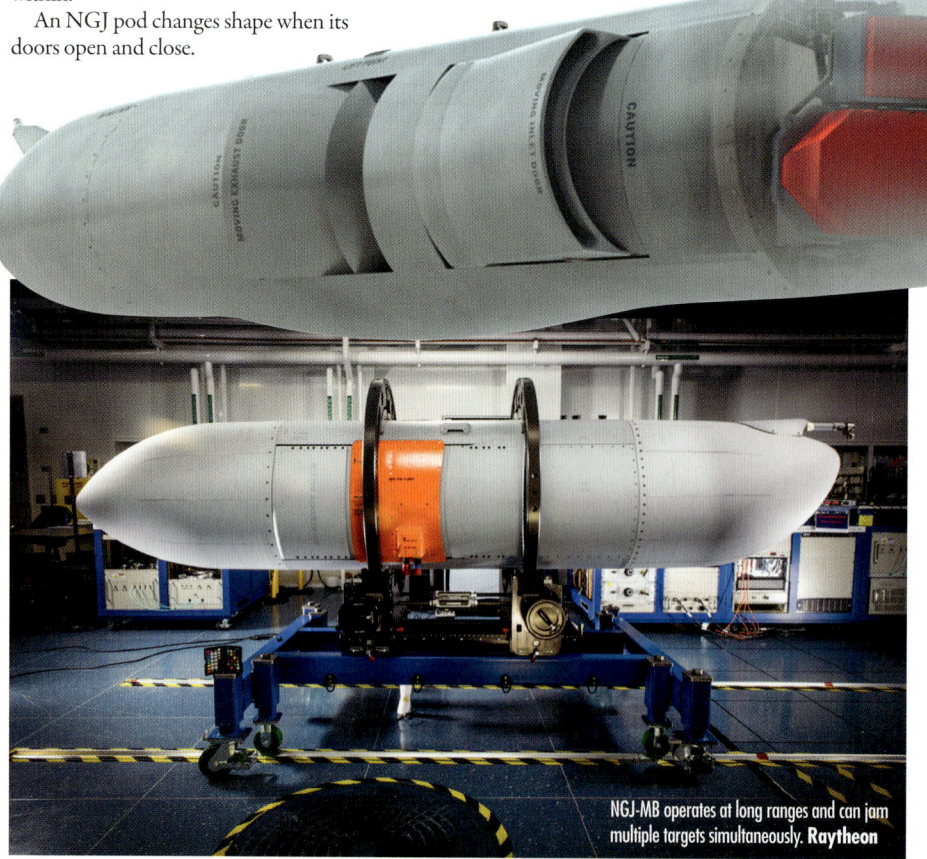

NGJ-MB operates at long ranges and can jam multiple targets simultaneously. **Raytheon**

Milestones

April 2016 was an important month for the NGJ-MB programme; it received Milestone B approval to enter EMD, and Raytheon was awarded a 56-month contract valued at US$1bn for execution of the EMD phase. In accordance with the contract, Raytheon will deliver 15 engineering development model pods to be used for mission systems testing and qualification, and 14 aeromechanical pods for airworthiness certification.

The NGJ-MB programme completed its critical design review on April 27, 2017, which identified deficiencies that deemed a redesign of the pod structure, which caused schedule and cost breaches to the programme. Despite the structure redesign development, manufacturing, integration and testing of the antenna arrays, power generation system, software, and common electronics unit continued, in accordance with the EA-18G high order language operational flight program H16 software integration schedule.

An EA-18G Growler loaded with a single NGJ-LB pod (centreline station) and two NGJ-MB pods, one on each underwing inner pylon, during May 2020. The aircraft is shown suspended inside NAVAIR's Air Combat Environment Test and Evaluation Facility at Patuxent River. **Naval Air Systems Command**

On August 31, 2020, NAVAIR concluded two demonstrations of existing technologies (DET) contracts, one with Northrup Grumman Corporation and one with L3Harris, for the NGJ-LB programme. The DET phase consisted of an assessment of technical maturity of the required technology to field the NGJ-LB capabilities. As of mid-August 2021, NGJ-LB completed its Milestone B review which enables the programme to enter its engineering and manufacturing development phase, which marked the start of the programme.

The NGJ-HB programme is still very early in the acquisition and no proposed designs have been selected for review.

The US Navy was originally scheduled to decide if the NGJ-MB programme was ready to proceed past Milestone C in September 2020. Programme delays prevented the completion of the ten development test flights required by the acquisition decision memorandum (ADM) to enter Milestone C. The delays were caused by several factors in addition to COVID-19, including late pod deliveries, complexity of test equipment integration, and initial manufacturing and quality issues discovered with the flight test deliveries.

Milestone C approval was received from Frederick Stefany, acting Assistant Secretary of the Navy for Research, Development and Acquisition on June 28, 2021. As with all weapon programmes, the Milestone C decision gave NAVAIR the green light to enter the production and deployment phase and start low-rate initial production.

At the time of the Milestone C decision, NGJ-MB pods had completed more than 145 hours of aero mechanical loads testing of the pod's physical integration on the aircraft; flying qualities flight testing; and mission systems testing of the pod's performance.

Additionally, NGJ-MB pods have clocked-up over 3,100 hours of ground testing at China Lake (chamber and laboratory) and Pax River (chamber).

The intent of the envelope expansion programme is to provide the fleet with the whole operating envelope of Growler when carrying two NGJ-MB pods. More broadly, the test programme seeks to verify the pod produces the power, jamming techniques, and beams it is supposed to, and functions in the entire frequency spectrum it is designed to operate in.

Achieving the programme's objectives is undertaken by multiple sites around the United States, not least VX-23's test team who write the test plans, build the test cards, and put in place all of the things required for each test mission flown.

Summing up the road-map ahead for the EA-18G Growler, Captain May said that PMA-265's focus is to deliver Growler Capability Modification aircraft to the fleet ahead of delivery of NGJ-MB pods. Similarly, Captain Dailey said there are many months of NGJ-MB developmental testing remaining, which will lead into initial operational test and evaluation, which will then lead to initial operational capability declaration currently planned for September of 2023.

EA-18G GROWLER

Mark Ayton details the training mission of Electronic Attack Squadron 129, the schoolhouse and repository of electronic attack in the US Navy.

WHIDBEY ISLAND IS located 30 miles north of Seattle in Washington State. It's farming country and a tourist destination. Quaint shoreline towns, beaches, forest, and lakes make the island idyllic. The largest city is Oak Harbor, three miles south of the island's largest employer, Naval Air Station Whidbey Island. The air station supports three tactical missions: signals intelligence gathering, maritime surveillance and electronic attack.

Two aviation wings are based at Whidbey Island. Patrol and Reconnaissance Wing 10 (CPRW-10) with six patrol squadrons operating the P-8A Poseidon maritime surveillance aircraft, one flying the P-3C Orion, and one aerial reconnaissance squadron flying the EP-3E Aries II signals intelligence aircraft. The other is Electronic Attack Wing Pacific (CVWP) with 14 electronic attack squadrons all equipped with the EA-18G Growler.

By official US Navy definition, electronic attack can be either jamming or deception. Jamming refers to the use of electronic transmissions to swamp a radar receiver and hide (technically conceal) the targets (friendly aircraft in the battlespace). Deception refers to the use of electronic transmissions to forge false target signals that a radar receiver accepts and processes as real targets.

Vikings

The largest aviation unit based at Whidbey is Electronic Attack Squadron 129 (VAQ-129) 'Vikings', the EA-18G Growler Fleet Replacement Squadron (FRS). Compared to an operational fleet squadron with five or six jets and 200 personnel assigned, VAQ-129 has 55 jets, 400 enlisted, 200 officers and 200 civilian personnel in its billet, and stands as the largest Growler squadron.

VAQ-129 has two missions that support each other. One is to train and graduate new crews to fill seats in the operational fleet squadrons. The other is to be the repository of personnel skilled in electronic attack and EA-18G aircraft for the CVWP and the operational squadrons.

For the seven-year transition period that concluded in April 2016, VAQ-129 was responsible for transitioning all 14 squadrons assigned to the CVWP from the EA-6B Prowler to the EA-18G Growler and teaching the operational squadrons to fly the new jet, which involved the qualification of 1,024 aircrew.

Growler School

VAQ-129 runs six classes per year. Each class comprises about 15 individuals enrolled on the multiphase, 52-week course designed for ensigns and lieutenants (junior grade) fresh out of flight school and without previous experience of flying the Growler.

Shorter courses are staged for lieutenant commanders returning to the Growler community and officers who are returning to complete their department head tour after completing the Prospective Commanding Officer Course or the Prospective Executive Officer Leadership Course at the Naval War College at Newport, Rhode Island.

Interestingly, student pilots and electronic warfare officers (EWOs) are paired up for the entire time. All instruction and training instils tactical crew coordination (TCC) as the mindset from the word go because pilots and EWOs will always fly together - the curriculum only differs for pilots who must fly a few extra events to learn more advanced handling characteristics of the jet.

Pilots arrive at VAQ-129 from a training squadron where they will have flown the T-45 Goshawk. Instructor pilots with VAQ-129

An EA-18G Growler and a B-1B Lancer assigned to the 28th Bomb Wing during a VAQ-129 detachment at Ellsworth Air Force Base, South Dakota. **US Air Force/94th Airlift Wing**

VIKINGS
THE GROWLER SCHOOLHOUSE

An EA-18G Growler receives fuel from a KC-135 Stratotanker during a training sortie from Naval Air Station Whidbey Island. **US Air Force/SSgt Julianne Showalter**

said the Growler is stable and an easy aircraft to fly, and that its flying properties are much the same as the T-45, though the systems are very different. The T-45 does not have afterburner, so the Growler has a lot more thrust and accelerates much faster. Along with its sheer power, a student must also get used to the Growler's sight picture which differs from the T-45.

The aircraft is equipped with HOTAS (hands-on throttle and stick) controls, which provide excellent ergonomics to the EWO and the pilot. The EWO uses two joysticks, each covered with switches and buttons, to control almost everything without the need to touch the cockpit screens. Similarly, the pilot can fly HOTAS and manipulate cursors to command most functions of the jet via menus.

Familiarisation

Like all other fast jet pilot training syllabuses, the Growler course starts with a basic familiarisation (FAM) stage, during which the student learns how to start up and shut down the engines and turn on systems. This is followed by the flight stage, during which the pilot learns how to fly the jet in accordance with the Naval Air Training and Operating Procedures Standardization (NATOPS) programme.

The very first FAM flight is flown in a Growler trainer (GT), a variant equipped with a stick and throttle in the back seat that the instructor pilot can use, if required. All subsequent FAM flights are flown with an instructor EWO in a standard Growler. That means the student is the only one with controls, though there is a nub set in the floor of the aft

US Air Force/SSgt Sandra Welch

cockpit at the position where the control stick is fitted when the aircraft is configured as a trainer. This is not used as a backup control but as a last ditch means for the EWO to use if the pilot is incapacitated for some reason.

Formation Flying

This second phase comprises just four flights, because the students have already done a lot of formation flying with their previous training squadron flying the T-45. They know the basics and understand the geometry and how it works.

Compared to the T-45, the Growler's different sight picture affects what they can see and how things look at the rendezvous with their wingman, as do the difference in power and how the aircraft responds and handles.

All four flights are flown in a standard jet with an instructor EWO who monitors the pilot's actions. The rendezvous and join up with other Growler aircraft are set by an instructor pilot, who watches the student join up with the formation from another jet to make sure nobody is outside of the parameters.

US Navy/Petty Officer 3rd Class Nathan Beard

Air-to-Air

The air-to-air phase accounts for 33% of the syllabus and covers all-weather intercepts (AWIs) and air-to-air counter tactics (AACT). It is introduced as a secondary mission but with a defensive mind set.

Within visual range (WVR) followed by beyond visual range (BVR) air-to-air combat are conducted with the understanding that if a Growler gets caught up in a WVR engagement the crew are fighting for their lives. Student pilots are instructed on the need for self-protection and not with a fighter pilot persona.

Being armed with two AIM-120 AMRAAM missiles helps a Growler crew to get closer to the fight, because they can protect themselves and it allows them to assume slightly more risk and provide better electronic attack support to the overall strike package. To match how Growler squadrons operate in the fleet, VAQ-129's air-to-air training comprises just two-plane engagements, and two-plane targeting.

In the AWI stage, students learn basic radar manipulation using the APG-79 AESA radar and how to use the radar to look at the geometry and rendezvous on another aircraft not part of their flight. In fleet operations a Growler pilot might be required to intercept an aircraft or fly alongside as an escort. One of the biggest challenges for a student pilot is learning how to interpret their radar's picture and determine how to manoeuvre their jet into a good position to rendezvous on another aircraft.

The AWI phase is the first time the student pilot flies an aircraft equipped with a radar; the T-45 Goshawk has no radar. By comparison, student EWOs do undertake radar training with their previous training squadron using the Virtual Mission Training System (VMTS), a very capable radar simulator in the T-45's aft cockpit. The VMTS generates a radar picture very similar to an APG-series system. In addition to the cockpit display, according to Boeing, a datalink allows an instructor on the ground to monitor virtual radar screens that mirror exactly what the student sees during flight. Sitting at a ground station (a computer terminal and screen), the instructor can simulate virtual air-to-air and surface-to-air scenarios to the student while in flight. During the debrief, the student is able play back and critique the session using a recording of the radar captured by the VMTS through the entire flight.

Students receive instruction on the APG-79 in what's referred to as radar mech, covering for example what's required to steer the radar to the proper sector of sky to look at the target.

VAQ-129 instructor pilots rate the APG-79 as easy to operate with its 4in x 4in display. Students are instructed on the way information is displayed by the APG-79 and how to interpret the target aspect (the angle between the major axis of the target's heading direction and the radar line of sight) and the radar picture.

US Air Force/Senior Airman John Linzmeier

EA-18G GROWLER

Smoke spools from the tyres as EA-18G BuNo 169137/NJ525 bounces on runway 14 during field landing carrier practice at Naval Air Station Whidbey Island. **Mark Ayton**

In the follow-on AACT stage, students learn about surface-to-air and AACT in the WVR and BVR environments. All sorties in the AACT stage are flown for self-defence purposes in which the student must remain at a longer range from the threat aircraft from where the AIM-120 AMRAAM is optimal. But because pilots must learn what to do in a WVR scenario, the first couple of flights involve flying counter tactics, manoeuvring the aircraft to suit. The scenarios involve two aircraft flying against each other at high speed and close range, and to the edge of its handling envelope, and are flown with an instructor pilot in a GT aircraft.

To support students in the AWI and AACT stages, VAQ-129 stages fighter detachments to Naval Air Station Fallon Nevada or Naval Air Station Key West, Florida.

Between AACT and the Airborne Electronic Attack (AEA) phase, student aircrew often fly sorties to practice aerial refuelling and low-level flying as part of the transition phase of the syllabus.

Airborne Electronic Attack

Airborne Electronic Attack (AEA) accounts for 50% of the syllabus and is by its very nature the biggest, most dynamic, and most difficult phase for pilots and EWOs alike. To succeed in the AEA phase, students must become very familiar with the display menus used to operate systems such as the ALQ-99 tactical jamming pod, ALQ-218 sensor system (encompassing a radar warning receiver, electronic support measures and electronic intelligence), the AGM-88 High-Speed Anti-Radiation Missile and the AGM-88E Advanced Anti-Radiation Guided Missile.

Task management is the biggest challenge for pilots and EWOs in the AEA mission set. The challenge is caused by the amount of information fed to the crew and their ability to determine the most important at the time and what can be ignored.

At this point in the story, it's appropriate to consider two aspects of AEA in the Growler. One, it's a two-seat aircraft compared to its predecessor, the four-seat EA-6B Prowler, and two, the consequential crew resource management and vital TCC chain required to undertake mission tasks with half the number of crew on board.

Generally, the Prowler was a harder aircraft to fly and less forgiving than the Growler. Consequently, the Prowler pilot assigned much more time to concentrating on flying the aircraft, whereas a Growler pilot has many more mission-specific tasks to do. However, thanks to pilot relief modes and auto pilot, the jet is easier to fly.

The TCC chain is a ladder of responsibilities assigned by priority to the pilot and the EWO. Pilot responsibility starts with safety of flight (making sure the aircraft is clear of other aircraft and in a good position for jamming), air-to-air picture (making sure there are no threat aircraft nearby), air-to-ground (making sure the aircraft is in the correct position for a HARM missile shot), electronic attack and electronic surveillance. The EWO's ladder starts with electronic surveillance and electronic attack and ascends the ladder in reverse order to the pilot.

The instructor sets up their displays and instructs the student where to place them to follow the TCC chain.

Typically, the pilot's display shows just positioning information and a good air-to-air picture, because the EWO is concentrating on the ground picture and making sure the right systems are set-up for jamming. Once the pilot has concluded with any air-to-air threats and HARM shots, they refer to a display that shows an overview of the jamming assignments and what power is coming from each jammer pod. The display is set up in an intuitive way that's easy to regularly glance at. This makes it easier for the pilot to advise the EWO of any power drop-off issues with any of the assignments. The EWO may not see the power drop off a pod while focused on pop-up threats, where the strike aircraft are heading, and that they are sufficiently covered.

Depending on the task and what other aircraft are with the Growler, a scenario can become very complicated very quickly for a Growler crew. When instructing aircrew, VAQ-129 instructors try to make the training situation as plain as possible, stressing the importance of positioning and staying in the right area to manage risk. If they are out of position, they could be within the range of the threat missile and outside of the Growler's allowable level of risk and could get shot down.

The EA-18G Growler is the only tactical jamming platform in the US inventory and is classed as a national asset. That's because there are only a limited number in the fleet. To comply with the ALRs, Growler crews position

An EA-18G Growler climbs away from runway 14 following a bounce during field landing carrier practice at Naval Air Station Whidbey Island. **Mark Ayton**

themselves further from the threat missile to remain outside the missile engagement zones dubbed range rings.

Such situations have occurred during training because the pilot may have been distracted and thinks the threat is somewhere else and takes no avoidance action until he or she realises they are in the range ring. That's a dangerous situation for the pilot who must fight their way out of the range ring. Keeping the plan straightforward is one of the most important aspects of training. Too complicated, and the plan makes it much harder for the pilot to keep the aircraft safe.

Explaining, a VAQ-129 instructor said: "That's why in the TCC chain, the pilot's number one priority is safety of flight, and number two is positioning. We always tell student pilots if there's too much going on [so-called task saturation] and you can't think of what else to do, put the jet in the right section of sky, so the EWO can do [his or her] job and get the jamming down range. That goes back to prioritising which tasks are important at which time, which is the main part of AEA."

According to the instructor, despite the Growler's level of automation, prioritisation is not one of them: "During our briefing we talk through the TCC chain. Pilots start at the top and work down. Based on the threats we have that day, we expect the pilot and EWO to meet right about in the middle. If there is a big air threat, the pilot will be focused on the air picture and not electronic attack and electronic surveillance. If, on the other hand, there is no air threat whatsoever, the pilot is probably going to be working further down the ladder.

Similarly, if there's a robust surface-to-air threat laydown, then the EWO will be focusing on electronic attack, their primary responsibility, but it's found at the bottom of the ladder. If the surface-to-air threat is basic and we are looking for one system, then the EWO will be able to work further up the ladder and into the air picture a little bit more, backing up the pilot on positioning."

The EWO's ability to advise the pilot depends on their level of experience. A very experienced EWO will drive a junior pilot around, if needed. Similarly, a senior pilot will advise an EWO on the status of each jamming assignment, especially those that need to be covered.

Explaining how VAQ-129 instructors tutor students about the switches and menus required in the AEA phase, the instructor said the basis for learning is found in standardisation bulletins issued by the Airborne Electronic Attack Weapons School (EAWS), call sign HAVOC based at Whidbey, part of the Naval Aviation Warfighting Development Center (NAWDC, pronounced NAW-DIK) based at Naval Air Station Fallon, Nevada.

HAVOC comprises highly qualified Growler Tactics Instructors, or GTIs, that form the tactical repository of the EA-18G community, developing the tactics that get the most out of EA-18G sensors and weapons. HAVOC's mission is also to train Growler aircrew and intelligence officers on those tactics during the Growler Tactics Instructor Course. This is a rigorous 12-week syllabus of academic, simulator, and live fly events that earn graduates the GTI designation - the highest level of EA-18G tactical qualification that is recognised across US Naval Aviation.

HAVOC develops tactics, evaluates diverse ways to employ the Growler for maximum effectiveness, and makes recommendations on how aircrew should set up their displays. As the training squadron, VAQ-129 has a standard way of configuring the displays and requires the students to use the recommendations issued by the HAVOC so they receive the appropriate information and take the proper actions. Once a pilot gains experience with their fleet squadron, they devise their own technique and display configuration.

VAQ-129's syllabus is split into two phases: AEA 1 and AEA 2.

AEA 1 is described above, while AEA 2 consists of graduation missions involving scenarios like those presented in training exercises staged by NAWDC at Fallon.

The scenario comprises a ground-based threat laydown, an opposing air threat and an objective for the strike package. Students plan the mission in the Joint Mission Planning System cell and then fly. The mission encompasses electronic surveillance, to determine what emitters are radiating so the students can devise which ones to target, look at the current laydown, understanding where the strikers are going to go, and perhaps recommend the strikers go somewhere else. Providing advice and recommendations to keep aircrews out of danger is one of the squadron's bread-and-butter tasks, often put to the test due to pop-up mobile emitters.

The pilot waits with his hands off the controls while the air refuelling probe is extended during pre-flight checks. **Mark Ayton**

All areas of electronic attack include flying with the jammers switched on, executing an AGM-88 HARM missile game plan and coordinating with the strikers. Additionally, VAQ-129 expects the students to deal with an air-to-air threat.

This serves as a near authentic experience for employing HARM missiles at the right targets and understanding the HARM dynamic when supporting a striker in a combat zone.

All graduation missions are flown on detachment to other bases to meet the requirement for extensive airspace and an emitter library that is not available at Whidbey.

Electronic attack is a specialised mission not only within the US Navy, but also across the Department of Defense, and the EA-18G Growler currently stands as the last TACAIR platform in the US Navy that is mission specialised. This enables VAQ-129 to stand as the absolute experts in AEA, so if a strike squadron needs to discuss beeps and squeaks or jamming, that is the squadron's forte. Consequently, VAQ-129 puts the students through ground school for two Airborne Aviation EW phases dubbed AAEW 1 and AAEW 2.

AAEW 1 instructs radar theory: how a radar detects something, aspects such as radar waves, polarisation and antenna attenuation, the electronic spectrum, foreign radar, and surface-to-air missile systems with details of their different pulse widths, frequencies, and scan types.

Despite theory that is deeper than students require, the AAEW 1 phase is designed to set the student's expectation that they are learning to be an expert. The goal is to ensure all Growler aircrew can advise any member of an air wing or a coalition strike package about electronic warfare or the HARM missile. AAEW 1 lays a foundation for Cat I students to learn how a radar works, how radars are becoming more agile, and why that makes a Growler crew's mission even tougher.

AAEW 2 instructs how the Growler affects the electromagnetic spectrum, how to keep it away from enemy threats while also employing it in an advantageous manner. AAEW 2 is also tailored to mission planning to counter specific threat systems from the Vietnam-era SA-2 Guideline (Soviet S-75 Divina) all the way up to an SA-21 Growler (Russian S-400 Triumph long-range surface-to-air defence missile system) and beyond.

Students go through the AAEW 2 phase immediately ahead of the AEA phase and instructs on why certain profiles of flying are important, and how moving a Growler around affects the overall coverage and aspect, and ultimately the effectiveness of protecting others and themselves as they fly into a surface-to-air missile envelope.

Students can become overwhelmed with the AAEW phases quickly, so the classes are not a one-time event. VAQ-129 provides a baseline understanding of radars and what effects Growler brings to the battlespace. Once aircrew go to their fleet squadron, they receive continuing education in the fleet, and when they start to prepare for their air wing work-up, the EAWS puts them through a ground school and give an update of all the threat systems that have emerged around the world during the 24 months prior to the schooling. In short, VAQ-129's AAEW courses build a generic academic foundation for follow-on academics that aircrew will have to undertake in the fleet.

Detachments in support of the AEA phase

EA-18G Growler BuNo 169137/NJ525 a second from touch down during a bounce. **Mark Ayton**

This shot of Viking 521 shows the configuration of antennas and blisters fitted to the aircraft, and the close proximity of the centreline fuel tank to the nose wheel landing gear. **Mark Ayton**

are made to Naval Air Station Fallon, Nevada, Ellsworth Air Force Base, South Dakota, and Mountain Home Air Force Base, Idaho. The three locations each have a large range equipped with threat emitters that allow students to practice working through and recognising signals gathered by the aircraft and then conducting electronic attack based on the threat presentation seen.

Given the crucial requirement for electronic attack in support of a strike mission, the author asked what kind of instruction students receive for working through a system failure when airborne. A VAQ-129 instructor said such an eventuality is a go/no-go situation. He said: "When we instruct on how to support a strike package based on the minimum requirements set out by the strike lead, we set the go/no-go criteria to cover the specific requirement, which usually involves a required number of HARM missiles, jammer pods and Growler aircraft. We plan our mission to that. During the flight, the instructors call out one or more jammer pods as failed, so the students must figure out how to coordinate; how they will rearrange the assignments between, say, two aircraft, and still cover the minimum requirement. "Instructors may strike out another asset, say, a Block 50 F-16C, leaving the students with fewer HARMs carried by the aircraft within the strike package to still cover what the strike lead wanted. We typically arrange that, so they lose assets but are still able to meet the go requirements, but we want to see how they rearrange things to still accomplish the mission."

Underlining how dynamic the electronic attack environment is, VAQ-129 instructors described how it constantly changes depending on what other assets are working with the Growlers, what the threat is, how the threat is changing and the air picture stating that there is no single good way to do it.

The final phase of the course is carrier qualification (CQ).

Electronic Warfare Officer Training

Student EWOs arrive at VAQ-129 as Naval Flight Officers (NFOs) fresh out of Undergraduate Military Flight Officer Training with Training Wing 6 (TW-6) at Naval Air Station Pensacola, Florida. Pilots and NFOs join VAQ-129's student pool and initially go through AAEW (see above).

From the start of the course, pilots must have a full understanding of the AEA mission and its objectives and to perform some tasks when the EWO is overwhelmed by assignments.

According to a VAQ-129 instructor EWO, even though the EWO has a specialised job to do, pilots must also have a good understanding of the mission as well: "Some instructor pilots with VAQ-129 came from the strike fighter community flying Super Hornets. Even though they are experienced pilots, we spool them up with a basic AEA syllabus to provide instruction on what the jet brings to the fight, what signals it picks up, and how such information looks on the displays, which is very different from the appearance on a Super Hornet's display."

EWO training teaches the basics of electronic surveillance and electronic attack, all building towards an ability to mission plan, as the IEWO explained: "At first this includes a lot of button-pushing, learning how to turn on the jammers and other systems working up to mission planning to support a strike package against

VAQ-129 typically flies its aircraft in a clean configuration during most phases of the course as shown by Viking 525. **Mark Ayton**

EA-18G GROWLER

US Navy training procedures dictate that an aircraft is chained to the ramp even when operating at a shore base like Whidbey Island as seen in this shot of Viking 504 during a crew change. Adherence to the chaining protocol ensures maintainers and flight crew meet flight deck operating requirements. **Mark Ayton**

The EA-18G Growler is equipped with the ALQ-218 wideband receiver system used for emitter identification location. The system's receivers are housed in the distinctive wingtip pods. **Mark Ayton**

a threat laydown and what their first concern should be. On ingress to the target area an EWO must try to take out some of the ground-based early warning systems. As the fighters and strike aircraft ingress into a threat area, the EWO shuts down the surface-to-air missile systems and maybe jams airborne enemy radars during the fight. They must also determine what surface-to-air missile systems are in the target area, what's important at this time of the fight, and recognise from a strategic and tactical level what their priorities are going to be at any given moment against any given threat."

The biggest part of the mission for an EWO is managing the jammers, making sure everything is set up, tweaking small jamming parameters, and focusing on either electronic surveillance or electronic attack. Consequently, one of VAQ-129's main objectives is to expose EWOs to as many types of mission as possible, such as a coalition strike over land and one launched from a carrier when part of a carrier air wing. The IEWO explained: "To prepare them as best as possible we want to ensure they fly maritime and land-based missions to give them an idea of what they will be expected to perform in the fleet. Once they arrive at their fleet squadron, they start the next bubble of their training, diving deeper into the tactics and really mastering the trade, VAQ-129 gives them the building blocks."

Continued Training

Most students graduate VAQ-129 as a Level 1, the official US Navy category given to those who successfully complete a syllabus for their first-tour in model, normally a newly designated Naval Aviator (NA), NFO or Replacement Aircrew (RAC). Successful completion of a training syllabus results in NATOPS qualification, but training and qualification continues throughout the individual's flying career.

Once individuals arrive at their fleet squadron, they commence their Growler Weapons Tactics Program (GWTP) and follow the Level 2 tactical crewman syllabus. During the Level 2 syllabus students undertake everything from mission planning through to debriefing of Level 3 events until they are ready to commence their own Level 3 mission commander syllabus, followed by the Level 4 instructor syllabus, and finally Level 5 which is reserved for graduates from the electronic attack weapons school.

Crew Resource Management

Training students in crew resource management begins with tuition and instruction on display management - becoming comfortable with the cockpit displays and making sure they are set up properly, so they receive the right information at the right time and learn how to use that information.

A VAQ-129 IEWO explained: "We try to throw as many things at them as possible, so that they learn what's important and what's not. In the event of a pop-up warning or a caution pop-up, is it affecting anything you are doing immediately? Is it the vul phase? Do you have to start focusing on that now? If you do not, put it aside and focus on making sure your jamming is set up or making sure at this point your HARM missile is ready to go. From an EWO management perspective, we must make them recognise what is important and what is not. Getting a student EWO familiar with the displays and the weapon systems helps to make the training environment less stressful, so learning is made easier."

Vul phase refers to the vulnerability period or the time the aircraft are away from base and vulnerable to harm.

Display Configuration

VAQ-129 and the fleet squadrons now use a more regulated doctrine for display set-up configurations for distinct types of electronic attack than in the early years, one that dictates a standard display set-up as opposed to personal preference for all students and junior aircrew.

Experienced EWOs use their own preferred set-ups. Some prefer to lock the map north up -

A VAQ-129 EA-18G Growler approaches the ramp of the USS *Harry S. Truman* (CVN 75). **US Navy/Mass Communication Specialist 2nd Class Tommy Gooley**

some like to have the map spin with them. Some like to declutter the display, so, for example, at a certain time of the flight only early warning emitters pop up. Choice is driven by the type and the phase of the mission. The IEWO said: "You can configure the displays on deck, which is superefficient, or if you are super clever you can use JMPS [Joint Mission Planning System] to pre-programme, such that when you switch between different mission phases, the jet automatically displays your pre-loaded preferences. Alternatively, you can configure the displays while airborne."

The JMPS provides the information, automated tools and decision aids needed to plan aircraft, weapon, and sensor missions rapidly and accurately. The system loads mission data into aircraft, weapons, and avionics systems.

Mission phases for an in-and-out strike flown from an aircraft carrier are pre-push (getting all aircraft in the same sector of sky); push (when all aircraft start to flow out, usually led by fighters to sweep the airspace); ingress (the point at which the strike package commits to the attack during which the Growlers are jamming enemy systems); and egress.

Missions flown by one of the four expeditionary Growler squadrons deployed to a land base have different phases and are much longer in duration. After launch, the jets go to a tanker and remain on call in an area of airspace ready to respond to a request from ground forces. A second air refuelling follows, to enable another on-call window before a final trip to the tanker and return to base. Protecting a strike aircraft launched from land bases and tasked with a predetermined strike involves similar phases to the one listed above.

Whatever the type of mission being flown, the EWO must spend lots of time heads-down interfacing with the displays to oversee how the jammers are set up. That's tough to endure over lengthy periods of time. Describing how a situation can change, the IEWO said that while things are running well the EWO can be

Combat payloads carried by the EA-18G Growler vary, and require the combined 44,000lb (196kN) of thrust to get airborne. Viking 521 is seen launching with full afterburner in a clean training configuration giving the pilot an easy take-off performance. **Mark Ayton**

An aviation machinist's mate shoots an EA-18G Growler assigned to Electronic Attack Squadron 129 (VAQ-129) on the catapult of the aircraft carrier USS *Carl Vinson* (CVN 70). *US Navy/Mass Communication Specialist 3rd Class Aaron Smith*

A VAQ-129 EA-18G touches down on the runway during field carrier landing practice at Boca Chica Field, Florida. Three out of the six runways at Boca Chica Field are painted to look like the decks of aircraft carriers. *US Navy/Danette Baso Silvers*

working the displays in support of the mission, then suddenly, without telling you, the pilot banks the aircraft because of an air threat: "When that happens you have to take a breather and look outside. It's a standard part of the brief, known as operational risk management for AEA missions. Display fixation occurs when an EWO gets stuck staring down watching the displays. Mitigation for that is to always look outside to help how you are feeling and to break from the display."

Mission Planning

Mission planning by student aircrew should always meet the requirements contained in the brief given to them by their instructors. It's important that each student studies and fully understands the flight objectives. Students plan the entire mission using JMPS and must ensure all the waypoints and the right emitter loads have been entered into the system.

Mission briefing covers everything students could possibly need to know and gives them an opportunity to ask questions before they fly. Upon their return from the flight, they go to a mission debrief and look through the cockpit tape recordings, which show which displays were used and when. In the words of one VAQ-129 officer: "Everything throughout the course and your flight career is learnt during debriefing."

Given the complexity of the electronic attack environment, the author was interested to know how mission planning is instructed to students as they start the AEA phase, and how much responsibility they have in putting a mission together, faced with the set of threats presented to them. A VAQ-129 instructor pilot responded that mission planning is the most important part of the AEA phase: "We give them basic scenarios, so the student gets a solid understanding of looking at the problem, knows what the resources are, where to reference information and to put a plan together. Students will never devise the best plan. There will always be problems with a plan, but the process of looking at the problem, knowing what the threats and assets are and putting together a cohesive plan is the biggest understanding they can learn during the whole AEA phase. Once they get to their fleet squadron, they will experience more robust presentations and will have experienced people who can show them specifics."

Viking Duty

VAQ-129's duty extends beyond its billets at Whidbey to meet the requirements of the Carrier Air Wing commanders and operational squadrons forward-deployed around the world. As the repository of experienced personnel and resources, if a forward-deployed jet goes down or if aircrew or maintainers are needed at another location, VAQ-129 supplies a replacement jet or maintainers or instructors to fill the hole.

A student pilot taxies Viking 554 from the VAQ-129 flight line- with wings folded in accordance with standard training procedures. **Mark Ayton**

There are thousands of requirements and it's a function of good leadership and discussions as to which ones VAQ-129 fills, because at some point every instructor, every maintainer that is sent to fill a hole somewhere, takes a hit on the squadron's production.

One example involves syllabus requirements that VAQ-129 can't undertake at Whidbey Island. The squadron can't go to carrier qualification anywhere other than Naval Air Station Oceana or North Island because that's where the aircraft carriers are. Likewise, VAQ-129 does most of its air-to-air training at Key West or Fallon because they have resident adversary squadrons, and for its bread-and-

An EA-18G Growler assigned to VAQ-129 undergoes inspection before launch from the aircraft carrier USS *Carl Vinson* (CVN 70). **US Navy/Mass Communication Specialist 2nd Class Zackary Alan Landers**

An EA-18G Growler assigned to VAQ-129 seconds from catching a wire on the flight deck of the aircraft carrier USS *Theodore Roosevelt* (CVN 71). **US Navy/Mass Communication Specialist Ryan Kledzik**

butter airborne electronic attack mission it must deploy to places like Fallon, Ellsworth, or Mountain Home. Each base has a range equipped with electronic emitters. These are essential, so students can train against them to learn how to use the Growler's systems in the art of electronic attack. As a result, any time the squadron conducts a detachment, maintainers and jets go. That creates a balancing act of how many maintenance shifts are worked if 100 people are on an aircraft carrier and another 100 are in Fallon, Nevada.

That's an example of the squadron being tri-sited which is a regular event during which the squadron typically adopts a single maintenance shift when everyone works on the same shift to achieve as much work as is possible in a 12-hour window. Single-shift maintenance limits VAQ-129's opportunity to produce sorties, especially during the summer months when it doesn't get dark until 9pm.

Carrier Qualification
Standing on the table at the back end of USS *Carl Vinson* (CVN 70), a pilot, holding a toughened phone to his right ear for radio communication, watches as an EA-18G Growler approaches the flight deck. Assigned to VAQ-129, the pilot's white vest identifies him as a Landing Signals Officer (LSO). As any aircraft approaches the flight deck, the LSO's job out on the table, the colloquial term for the LSO platform, is to focus complete attention on the pilot flying the approach to make sure of a safe landing.

Ever since the first flight deck operation on board USS *Langley* in 1922, LSOs have been an essential part of the aircraft landing process. Until aircraft carriers were equipped with optical landing systems, an LSO held coloured flags or paddles to communicate directly with the pilot on approach to the flight deck. Today's LSOs continue to be dubbed paddles; their role on VAQ-129 or any other FRS is to prepare student pilots to do their first hack, a term used for the first carrier landing in a US Navy carrier-borne aircraft.

All student pilots on VAQ-129 first carrier qualify (CQ) in the T-45 Goshawk while assigned to their previous training squadron, but their course colleagues training to become electronic warfare officers (EWOs) have no previous experience of the carrier environment.

One VAQ-129 LSO said: "It's different enough for the pilots doing it in a grey aircraft, but it's a completely new experience for the EWOs. That adds another level to their relationship with the paddles and is much different [from how] it is in the fleet. A lot more time is spent getting them ready because they have no experience."

Explaining the preparations involved in preparing VAQ-129 students for their first carrier trap, the LSO said the process takes about six weeks: "On their training squadron the student pilot is led out to and back from the carrier by an instructor. The student's only job out there is to land. On VAQ-129, we teach them how to get to and from the ship, so they can take off, fly out, get over the ship and come back on their own. We provide lots of lectures on how to do that and how to fly an approach to the ship: the building blocks of how to do everything required. Then we start simulator training and FCLPs [field carrier landing practice]. Students do seven sims involving 35 approaches at night and about 140 passes before they go to the ship, so lots of practice landing in

the sim and the jet during the day and at night. Throughout the course, students get multiple chock talks and lectures about how things are done out at the ship."

Typically, VAQ-129 strives to crew each jet heading to the carrier for CQ with a student pilot and student EWO. The squadron LSO said there are plenty of eyes on the aircraft as it approaches the flight deck, in the tower and on the LSO platform: "But ultimately they are on their own. Any time an aircraft is behind the ship and you're on the table, all your attention is on that pilot to make sure they get on board safely. Our priorities don't change from the fleet to what we do with a student pilot, the difference being a student pilot is a little more unpredictable. We know they are going to deviate more than a fleet pilot; we don't know how, so we have to jump on the radio and give the pilot correction instructions."

According to another VAQ-129 LSO, landing signals officers acquire the skill set required for the job by watching thousands of passes on the ship and even more at the field: "As a new LSO, you have to see a lot of passes to recognise the deviation of the aircraft. It's all about repetition, that's all it is."

Both the Growler and Super Hornet can fly what are known as mode 1 approaches during which the aircraft is coupled to the automatic approach system until touchdown. The jet lands itself with the pilot monitoring to make sure it maintains the glideslope all the way down. Another semi-automatic landing mode is auto throttles, in which the pilot makes control stick inputs, but the throttles manage themselves with monitoring by the pilot.

Throughout their time with their training squadron and FRS, students are not allowed to use any type of automated approach mode. Everything a student pilot does on 129 is old-school manual, which allows the LSOs to judge if the student has successfully learned and accomplished the task of safely landing the aircraft on the flight deck.

To achieve carrier qualification, a pilot must achieve ten traps and two touch and goes in daytime, and six traps and two touch and goes at night. This quota usually takes two days to complete, because a student is restricted to ten daytime and four night-time traps in a 24-hour period.

One LSO assigned to VAQ-129 said the process ideally takes two days: "We like to get six daytime and the first four night traps done on the first day, followed the next day by four more daytime and two more night traps and the student is carrier qualified. It doesn't always work out that way because we run out of deck time. CQ can be a long evolution, some students take ten hours in the seat [the time required to get checked out], and others achieve it with two hours."

VAQ-129 LSOs and instructors expect a 100% completion rate for each trip to the boat, but that's just an expectation. If a student does not CQ or is disqualified (DQ) on the first boat trip, he or she returns to 129 and trains up again for the next boat. All students get two attempts to CQ.

Not all students who receive a DQ do so at the carrier, as one LSO explained: "A field DQ is another option. As we monitor a student's progress through the syllabus and before the boat, if we feel the student is not safe to fly behind the boat or requires more time, we can hold them back. That helps prevent people setting up for a failure.

"There are different ways of disqualification,

EA-18G GROWLER

A view of an EA-18G Growler captured through night vision goggles. **US Navy/VAQ-129**

boarding rate and grade plan average are the most common failure metrics. Each pass is graded and recorded. If a student forgets to bring the power up to mil power once they make the trap, that student gets a DQ on the grounds of safety; if the hook misses the wire, the aircraft is unlikely to be able to get airborne again, because the power setting is too low."

In the event of a DQ, the student must discuss CQ evolution with the instructors before starting training for the next boat. Managing the feelings and emotions of a student who has received a DQ is all a question of psychology and represents the greatest skill each LSO must learn. One VAQ-129 LSO said: "You have to find out how the student is feeling and figure out what they need to hear from you and that ability comes from repetition in the process."

The LSO in charge and an assistant for each boat trip spend considerable time with the students as they work up to CQ, learning about their personalities and what they need to hear from the LSOs before they go out. The LSO concluded: "You are part psychologist during that time."

Once students have achieved CQ, they are posted to one of the 14 fleet squadrons based at Whidbey Island. Throughout their time on VAQ-129, student pilots are dubbed nuggets; a title they keep until they have completed 50 traps with their fleet squadron. And as for the automatic and semi-automatic landing modes discussed earlier, at this point in their flying career with 50 traps under their belt, pilots are for the first time allowed to use automated landing modes.

All US Naval Aviators are tremendously talented people and those who operate from ships, not least aircraft carriers, have the additional stress of recovering to a flight-deck sometimes under inclement weather conditions with a pitching deck and at night. Weather does not discriminate between types of aircraft: EA-18G aircrews face such recovery conditions at the end of long missions during which they have undertaken the complexities of the electronic attack for hours at a time. It is energy sapping work. To meet the demands of their tasked missions, all Growler aircrew count on the training provided during the year-long course run by the Vikings of VAQ-129.

An aviation electronics technician assigned to VAQ-129 inspects the tail hook of an EA-18G Growler on the flight deck of the aircraft carrier USS *Theodore Roosevelt* (CVN 71) on September 25, 2020. **US Navy/Mass Communication Specialist Dylan Lavin**